In a
MW00882251
Shalom Blessing

FROM HOOD TO GOOD

GERALD MIDDLETON

PRESS

Table of Contents

Special Dedication to the Readers

Fʀᴏᴍ Hᴏᴏᴅ Tᴏ Gᴏᴏᴅ

Forward

EARLY YEARS

*I*n the early years J. grew up on mean streets in the hood of New Jersey. He was the oldest sibling of four boys, J. never knew his birth father until he reached the tender age of fifteen, and yet, he still had many unanswered questions to his life.

J. was an angry and resentful man growing into his late teens up to his early adulthood years. He was known for his lack of trust from his hood, his family, and his women. J. was known in New Jersey, as one who took matters into his own hands. J. was going to get things done, by his own method of thinking. Hence his street name Double-o-Seven-007 which wasn't given to him for any reason.

J. life experience in New Jersey is intense. This book shares his journey of his family life trials, struggles, triumphs, celebrations and even his greatest victories!

From Hood to Good, is electrifying! It is raw! It's just real talk! His Part One experience will captivate his readers. J. shares intimate details about his home relationships, his two brothers (one who was dealt with a gruesome death), and one who was sentenced to more than one hundred fifty years in prison, as well as knowing someone who is serving fifty years. J. shares his reason, motives, and desires for getting into the fast life, the streets, and its destructive game. What becomes of J. in the hood of New Jersey? Who will be next to live or die in his hood. J. is very brave and courageous as he allows you to experience his whirlwind of life.

This book, From Hood to Good, is a True Best Seller! After reading Part One both you and I as his readers, will not want to wait much longer for the sequel!

Experience a Rush of a Great Read! You are invited to enter From Hood to Good.

Special Dedication to the Readers
From Gerald Middleton

$\mathscr{F}$irst I would like to give God all the Glory and the Honor for giving me this gift that he has placed inside of me, in writing this book. As I embark in opening my life story to all readers from all areas of life, I would like you all to know that yes this book is based on a true story but the <u>truth</u> is that I am a brand new person in Jesus Christ. This can apply to you the reader as well.

From Hood to Good Part One and the follow up sequel both speak about real life experiences that someone might be going through today. However from my heart to yours, I pray that you would allow the Lord to come into your life and change you just as he has changed me.

Romans 12:1, 2 AMP.

- (verse 1) *I appeal therefore to you brethren, and beg of you in view of (all) the mercies of God, to make a decisive dedication of your bodies (presenting) all of your members and faculties (as a living sacrifice) holy (devoted, consecrated) and well pleasing to God, which is your reasonable (rational, intelligent) service and spiritual worship.*

- (verse 2) *Don't not be confirmed to this world (this age), [fashioned after and adapted to its external, superficial customs] but transformed (changed) by the [entire] renewal of your mind [by its new ideals and its new attitude] so that you may prove [for yourselves] what is the good and acceptable perfect will of God, even the thing which is good and acceptable and perfect [in his sight for you].*

- *Basically the above is stating that change comes by you constantly allowing God to renew your mind to the word of God.*

From Hood to Good is a life journey experience! Things that I have experienced in my past, you as the reader may have gone through certain similarities in your life as well. One thing that I want you to understand as you read and experience <u>From Hood to Good</u>, is insight in knowing that God has a plan and a big bright future for you in your life.

Jeremiah 29:11 NIV

- For I know the plans I have for your, says the Lord. They are plans for good and not for disaster, to give you a future and a hope.

As I look back on my life, I see my life story as being like Joseph in the bible. There is a scripture that reads in Genesis 50:20 KJV

- But as for you, you thought evil against me; but God meant it unto good, to bring to pass, as it is this day to save much people alive. What the enemy meant for evil, God still meant it for good.

CHAPTER 1

THE TABLE

I remember like it was yesterday, sitting at the table getting ready to head off to school when AD, Peanut, Poochie, and I was eating Apple Jacks laughing and arguing over wearing each other shirts and pants. My mom was yelling in the background telling us to quiet down and hurry up so we wouldn't be late for school.

Man, I don't want to go to school, one of us would always say. Then my mom would come in and put the finishing touches on us. Even though we did not have much, our mom worked with what she had at the time. She showed us the best love she could give which was she.

Our living conditions were hard compared to some. I can recall the times when we used cooking butter for our faces when we ran out of regular hair grease.

The winters, wow!. One time when it was very cold out, the inside of our house was freezing because we did not have any heat. This reminds me of our poor little fish that were frozen in the fish tank. I will never forget that particular winter when it took AD forty-five minutes from leaving the house and going to our favorite pizza spot. We were so hungry, and we were excited about getting some pizza but by the time AD got back both him and the pizza were frozen.

I laugh and smile at these memories now but while going through those times, it made me feel like, *man there has to be something better than this*! However, my brothers and I did not know what that was, so we adapted to it. This was life as we knew it.

As a kid growing up I liked to dress and I always had to have my hair looking tight. Despite how fresh I liked to look, I had to keep it honest with my mom. I dreaded and hated the fact that my mom used a straighten comb on my head! I enjoyed my afro. It got to the point where I did not care anymore, and it was that bad. I said to her, *"Mom just get me a Jerri Curl since my name was Jerry anyway."*

My brothers had their choice and it was haircuts. Mine, on the other hand, was sporting my new Jerri Curl. I rolled in style wearing my bell-bottoms, button collar shirt, and of course the red and blue Pro-Keds. Man, I was sharp!

As I was growing up in my town, and I am sure if any other kid wanted to compare his household with mine he would say that his household was normal and functional. Well mine on the other hand was the farthest thing from normal! However, it was what we knew and understood "normal" to be.

With the love from my mom and my bond from us brothers, we all were a force to be reckoned with. With a dad who was back and forth, being in and out of our lives, and when he did stay around long enough for us to see him his presence in the house made my brothers and I fearful. None of us wanted to get on his bad side, especially me. So I would make sure I was on the up and up, staying on his good side.

He was one strict man and he did not take any mess! I can speak for all of us on how he laid down the law; he gave us his house rules. He would give the chores we had to do, and he strongly encouraged us to abide by them or else! I made sure, I did whatever needed to be done, so I would not need to see the "or else". If any of us would get out of line, man we all would get it! He would to hold us up by the leg and give us an "ole fashion down south beating" as he would call it. He would get that way with us at times . . . he would make me always ask questions to myself Those questions would be like "*What really happened* to him?" or "What made him that angry?" or "Why would he tick off like that?" I simply do not know if he was angry from his past or what.

Just as he was tough on us in the house, he was so much tougher on the streets! He was well known for getting major paper, his women and dressing sharp as a tack. I remember his snakeskin, lizard and of course his gator shoes. Those looking on the outside in, they would say he was untouchable. Yeah, that's right, untouchable. I guess it was true. It was one of his favorite movies and he would watch it when he was at home.

As I got older, I would hear people tell me that *your dad was no joke*! He had mad respect on the streets. He had his stint of his crimes, his gangster ways, which would have him on the run.

I always remember taking the family trips to Philly, *if that is what you want to call them*. He would always give us a code to use at the door. This way, he would know it was us at the door rather than the boys in blue. Once inside, he was sure to ask us how we were doing in school, and at home. He had his unique way of showing us how much he cared. He would give us money for school shopping and boy oh boy how happy were we.

Aside from him getting major paper on the streets, he was getting his groove on as well. It was sad to see his life going in this direction. I knew for sure something was wrong when my brothers and I were frying some chicken one day. We did not have any flour but we were hungry so we fried the chicken just as it was in some hot grease! We almost burned the house down, the kitchen was full of smoke, we were yelling telling each other what to do, and laughing. In the midst of all this commotion, my dad was so on and he was out of it! He did not even smell the burnt chicken or notice the smoke.

Despite the relationship my mom had with him, she continued to stay in focus! In her eyes, you could see it, she was going to do something better and positive. My mom had enrolled in nursing school. She was going to school and doing well. Just when things started to begin turning around for my mom... her mom passed, but my mom just kept on going. She never quit. She was so determined to make it. In addition to caring for her youngest brother, my uncle Lawrence, I recall how she would walk from our house to nursing school despite the rain, snow and heat. With no car at that time, she continued to go to school and graduated as a registered nurse.

Even though she was working long hours as a nurse, my mom enjoyed company and she loved to entertain both family and friends. She insisted that her house was always staying neat and clean! I remember one weekend my aunt came by with my two little cousins and she asked my mom if she could baby-sit for her.

My mom told her yes, but my aunt never came back to pick them up. So they began living with us as my mom raised them and took care of them as they were her own. We all formed a bond of becoming brothers and sisters. Some years later, we found out that my aunt had passed away. She was a beautiful person with a warm and pleasant personality. Still standing strong my mom went on raising six kids. Talk about minor lifestyle adjustments!

CHAPTER 2

LIFE ADJUSTMENTS

We were all growing up struggling. My mom was going to school and with her limited work schedule; it resulted in us going on welfare so using food stamps came in handy. With all of this tension, my mom still wanted some type of social life.

One can only imagine how good it would be to go out to socialize and mingle with other adults who understand adult things. Working, going to school and raising six kids, I understand now how much my mom really needed a break.

Back then, none of us could understand it! We made it hard for her. We tied up one of our first baby-sitters, put tissues in his toes, set them on fire when he dozed off to sleep. He quit! The next baby-sitter came and went. We even threw batteries out of the windows. We threw water out onto the streets onto people and one of the favorite things that we enjoyed doing to the baby-sitter was jumping them when they got out of line. We were off the hook! My mom was known around town for some bad kids and no one wanted to baby-sit for her. When she would ask some people from the neighborhood, they were very quick in telling her how busy they were and of course, the famous quote was that they already had something to do.

Eventually she had some of her nephews baby-sit for her. Of course, they had their own rules. In particular was that they did not want to hear it and if anything went down as far as us making too much noise, they would separate us.

I remember when my mom decided that she wanted to date. We all sprang into action quickly. My brothers and I came up with plans and ideas to keep these men away from our mom. We just wanted her to ourselves. Therefore, when the men came around, we gave them cold stares. We would purposely eat everything that we had in the house. Doing stuff like this caused these men think twice. We knew exactly what they were thinking... *we cost too much*. Ha! As far as my mom dating, eventually that happened when we all got much older. *She got the hint*.

When I was fifteen, I remember the day when I was in school and one of my schoolmates came to me and said that my dad said to call him. I was like, 'what'? My dad isn't with my mom but he is right here in town? She said no, that is not your real dad! Your real dad goes out with my older sister.

Here is the phone number, as she wrote in on a piece of paper. She said that he said give him a call, his name is Gerald and you are little Gerald. I think she was happy that I was going to finally find out who my dad was. Completely floored, confused, shocked, and stunned …. I cried.

With tears in my eyes, I ran home to ask my mom what was going on. Who and why would my school-mate come and hand me this phone number and tell me that my real dad said to call him and that I am little Gerald?

I wanted answers! I demanded answers! I needed to know and understand what was going on. What was wrong? Who was I … who is this man … who is my dad? The man, that I knew all my life was my dad. Or was he? So who is Gerald? And why am I little Gerald?

No words, from my mom. Quiet and still. She said, "What are you talking about, and who told you this?" I found out, that's what I told her. My mom said, "Found out what?" "The truth" is what I said! And I ran away, jumped on the local college campus bus and rode all night long thinking back and forth. I rode and rode that bus … just staring off and thinking … What is going on? Why me?

Well, I didn't have time to figure it out. I was now on the block, hanging out with my homies. I was getting the love and dap from them. That's the one thing that I needed and wanted most was love. Why not from the block?

Meanwhile, my uncle Lawrence found me from the time I ran away and handed me a letter saying that it was from my mom. With a hurt and disgusted attitude I took the letter knowing what I know now: "hurt people, hurt people." Later on after taking it down, I read the letter my mom wrote. She explained it as this:

Dear Jerry,

Some things went down in the past. Your real father was not always there, when my mom passed he wasn't there for me and I didn't know what to do.

Your dad and I went thru some things before I met your step-dad. Your real father and I didn't work out. Your real father cheated on me, he also left for the armed forces and I moved on with my life. I was going to tell you but didn't know how. I would like to ask you to forgive me and I'm sorry.

Love Mom.

CHAPTER 3

THE PHONE CALL

*S*o moving on, I contacted my real father. I went to a pay phone off the block of Georges Road and made the call. When the phone rang there was an answer, it was my father's voice. I recall the conversation as....

Gerald–(father speaking) …. Hello

Jerry–(me speaking)…. Hello, who is this?

Gerald–this is Big Jerry

Jerry–this is Jerry

Gerald–who little Jerry?

Jerry–Yeah!

Gerald–Aaahh man, good to hear from you... I haven't talk to you in a long time

Jerry–What's going on? A young lady in my homeroom class gave me your phone number and told me you were my father?

Gerald–Yeah, I am your father.

Jerry–*my heart dropped* when he told me he was my father ... I was hysterical! I said, "You're my father?"

Gerald – Yes.

Jerry–What's going on man?

Gerald–I'm your father and I want to see you.

Jerry–I said that I always knew something in my heart that the man that raised me was not my real father. I felt it! Something on the inside of me especially my heart knew but I just couldn't place it.

Gerald—His response was "Yeah man. I am your father and I want to see you. I waited until you got older so I could tell you. I used to see your mother all the time at the Elks or at the bar and I would say to her when are you going to tell little Jerry about me? She would say that she was going to tell you. But she never did. So I made it my business to tell you at this time."

Now, as I reflect back on this conversation as an older and wiser man, it puts me in the place of where the scripture tells about <u>Time</u>. Ecclesiastes 3 verses 1-8:

To everything there is a season, and a time to every purpose under heaven. Verse 2: A time to be born and a time to die. A time to plant, a time to pluck up, that which is planted. Verse 3: A time to kill, and a time to heal, a time to breakdown, a time to build up. Verse 4: A time to weep, a time laugh, a time to mourn, a time dance. Verse 5: A time to cast away stones, a time to gather stones together, a time to embrace, a time to refrain from embracing. Verse 6: A time to get, a time to loose, a time to keep, a time to cast away. Verse 7: A time to rend, a time to sow, a time to keep silence, and a time to speak. Verse 8: A time to grow, a time to love, a time to hate, a time to war, a time of peace.

And this was <u>MY TIME</u> to be loved by my real father!

Now I sit and think of the meaning of the word <u>time</u>. It means the concept of continuous existing, the past, the present, and future. Time also means, relating to; payable at a future date. God already had a future date as to when I was to meet my real father. God is good. Amen.

CHAPTER 4

OUR FIRST MEETING

*T*he arrangements were made and we met. My father came to pick me up from the corner of where I spoke to him on the pay phone. I was ready and I was excited! Although he told me fifteen minutes, he was there in what felt five to ten minutes, he must have been excited too.

My father pulled up at the corner where I was standing. He is driving a Cadillac Coupe de Ville shiny brown, waxed and buffed – man, it glistened like a diamond! My reaction and words with expression were, "Man my father has some style." As for growing up in the hood and recalling how my mom struggled with her five boys and one girl–then I see my dad in this Caddie–he looked like he was a millionaire–he had it going on.

I recall him rolling down the window. He says: "Hi little Jerry, get in." I hurried in the car, shut my door and then I looked at my father. It was a direct reflection of me. I was looking at myself in the mirror. He said as he was reaching out towards me. "Heeey man, give me a hug". I responded with a hug and for the first time, I heard my real father tell me he loved me. I felt joyful like a puzzle being fixed. I was startled and still didn't have an understanding of what was going on, especially when he said "I love you." I just wanted to get down to the bottom of things. I wanted and needed answers.

My father asked if I was hungry and I was, so we went on our way to get something to eat. We went to a Burger King that was about two miles up the road. Once we got there, my father and I walked inside, ordered our food and I am just looking at him thinking to myself as I soak it all in, "Wow this is my dad, my real father." So we went and sat down at the table and ate our food. We began to talk. He was looking at me and saying that I had his full lips with the crease in the center, his dark brown eyes, and in a laughing manner he said, "You know have your mother's nose." Laughing with him I said to myself 'that's right'.

He went on and asked me how was school going—what grade was I in—what did I plan to do in my life. I responded, "I don't know, I am only 15." I think he understood that. He was excited to see me and asked how my mom was doing and I said she was doing fine.

My father said "Well, since you have seen me I'm not too sure how your mom will react." So I chuckled, laughed and said, "I don't know how either." But I knew it would be interesting.

So we finished eating our food. I was grinning, happy, and elated about meeting my real father. He had it together. He looked like a business man. After just learning that he went to college and graduated with a Business Degree from Rutgers College, I knew for sure he was! He dropped me back off at home and said that I could call him and come and see him anytime! He gave me the address to where he lived. He reached out again and gave me a big hug. I was so HAPPY! I felt confident. I felt loved. I felt good. I was smiling because for the first time in my life at this very present moment, the missing puzzle piece was just found.

CHAPTER 5

NEW AWAKENING

*S*o, I returned home and spoke to my mom about the time I just shared with my father, my real father–Big Gerald. She was fine with that. I think she was relieved that the weight was off her shoulders. I said, "So now I want to go live with my father, so I can get to know him." My mom said that was fine if that's what I wanted to do. "I have taken care of you all of these years."

I told her, "Yes, I want to live with my father–it's nothing against you, I just want to get to know him." Several weeks passed and I said good-bye to my mother. I was going to live with my father and man I was happy.

A new day had dawned, I moved from Georges Road to Power Street. It was totally different from where I just came from. On Georges Road I saw crime and drug dealers, all relative to the hood but on Power Street; I saw that my real dad had his own house. It is amazing, as to what you see when you turn the corner.

It was like the hood was in the rear view mirror and the dawn of the morning sun; my new awakening was in front of me. So stepping inside my new house, I met my grandmother. My father was taking care of her and grandma was no joke. I recalled my first encounter with her. She was slim and sort of tall for a lady and had a midwestern accent. My father said to his mom; "Mom, this is little Jerry" and she said "Let me check you out." I went to her; she looked at me and said, "He favors you." So from there, it was settled. I was little Jerry, Big Jerry's son.

Well, my dad went into quick action. He laid the ground rules, gave me my chore duties and he went over what he expected from me. I was still in awe of being in a house, seeing my real dad in the flesh, getting looked over by my grandma and now he was talking about rules. I was not used to that. I thought this was going to be different and it was. Fast forwarding, I recall cutting grass one day and man it was hot! I will never forget that summer day. Grass was flying everywhere, the sun was beaming down and I was really thirsty. I was sixteen and had thoughts of doing other things. So when my dad came and asked me how things were going, I said everything was fine. I told him that I left the lawn mower running in the back, and it was cutting the grass, not me. It was too hot. I disliked discipline, even though it was good for me.

Now, one thing I did like was money. So, my father worked out a deal with me. He paid me $1.00 for each of his dress shirts that I ironed. During the course of getting his shirts ironed, my father was teaching discipline and responsibility. He would tell me in order to make money you had to do positive things. Ironing his dress shirts was something good and honest and getting paid was a reward for my hard work. So, I would make sure that I ironed at least thirty shirts, because I knew I would get $30.00. I was catching on quick and getting wiser by the moment.

I remember when it was time for me to learn how to drive. My father said, "Ok Jerry, I am going to teach you how to drive". He told me to get in his driver's seat. I said, "Really, you are going to let me drive." He said, "Yeah." I was excited. I remember pushing the pedal to the metal. My father quickly told me "Take it easy on the pedal! Remember Jerry, it's a Caddie, and it's supposed to glide." Wow, I smile at those memories.

With the good times there were also times when I didn't want to do what my dad told me. So at those times I reached back out to my mom. I when I would call my mom to try to have her side with me, my mom reminded me that this is where I said that I wanted to live. She said that discipline was what I needed, and to listen, and she was right.

CHAPTER 6

REUNITED FORCE

*E*ntering in my senior year of high school my mother and father reunited after seventeen years of separation. My mother and father got back together. My father must have really loved my mother and us. He went and bought us a brick house in the suburbs and we all experienced something new again for the first time, a house that was ours to keep. I had a new sense of hope because I saw how much they still loved each other and for the first time we all were going to be a family together.

My brothers and I were adjusting to our father being in our lives and we were of the age where my father said we had a choice to make: either go to the army or get a job. We made a choice to get a job. Now, this wasn't the regular nine to five job like most people had or wanted. My brother and I on the other hand wanted a quick fix. Sure money, the dividends. So we began to hit the streets, living the fast life which was the game of destruction. My brother and I had the game sewn up. Within the course of two years we had our city on lock down.

There were beefs with some guys in regards to location. We battled back and forth for position. Who had the most blocks, the runners, and the best product? Ours was famously known as "the comeback" and believe me, the customers kept on coming back. Which caused the mumps in our pockets because of the cash flow we were getting paid.

I can recall when we made over three thousand in paper one day. The name of one of the famous streets in the hood was changed to Macy's Boulevard. It was full of street shoppers. Now that I look back on it, I realize how sad the life was that we chose to take. Being young and naïve and not fully understanding the impact of this new type of lifestyle, made it difficult to see how it was directly transforming us on the inside. We had mad paper, women, and endless cars. I remember when we would pay straight cash for the cars. Our duffle bags would be full of paper. We had a two door coupe Jaguar, Ford Mustang, Chevy Blazer, and a Ford Convertible 5.0 that had a mean drop top with fancy rims. You know the ones the Dayton's, and of course the Caddie that glide.

I remember when my younger brother and I were on the streets all night. I put the word out that we had rock the block, because we were going to get a new whip in the morning. We did just that: we broke day and got the new car. We were so loaded with cash that the sales man actually fell off his seat when he saw that type of paper.

Needless to say, when you live this type of fast life, it only leads you to a world of destruction. I say that now because I am a wiser man who is born again, with the mind of Christ, who has experienced some things. It reminds me of the scripture from Proverbs 14 verse 12 (King James Version) which speaks to destruction. It reads: *There is a way which seemeth right to a man, but the end thereof are the ways of death*.

I enjoy that particular scripture but it gives one a deeper understanding if you read it from the New Living Translation—Proverbs 14 verse 12 says: *There is a path before each person that seems right, but it ends in death*. What my brother and I were doing may have seemed right but it led us to a world of destruction and death!

Word of Wisdom–About Choices:

We have to be careful of the choices we make in our life because these choices will always bring a result. There are never any short-cuts in life. The path that seems right may offer many options and require a few sacrifices. Easy choices however should make us take a second look and ask ourselves "is this solution attractive because it allows me to be lazy" or "because it doesn't ask me to change my lifestyle", or simply "because it requires no moral restraint?" The right choices often require hard work and sacrifices. Do not be enticed by apparent short-cuts.

When I mention a world of destruction I will explain it as this ... as my brother and I got heavier into the game we had paper coming in, we went to other nearby states, we had to check and regulate on things and deal with them if they didn't come out correctly. Since we were well-known in the streets, we had to maintain it. As we got larger and larger, we experienced a life of fear and greed. The ***fear was*** the consequences of being caught and the ***greed was*** being addicted to getting that paper. How much paper? Major paper! Along with the major paper comes major pain and destruction.

CHAPTER 7

BOOT CAMP ....
FRONT AND CENTER

"*M*iddleton you are in." as I remember my recruiting officer sharing the good news. The United States Army front and center! Wow, who would have ever thought? Not me! I was ready to go make a man out of myself, my father was proud.

Although this was going to be a different change for me, I could not resist the fact that my little daughter was on the way. In the words of my father, the only honorable thing to do was to marry her. This was not what I had in mind.

Needless to say within my departing week I was getting married. I recall the wedding ceremony as such. My father arranged everything. He had the people, the food, the décor and all of the fixings. During the ceremony I heard her say "Yes" and when it was my turn to exchange my vows, I said "No". I felt pressured that this was something being forced upon me.

During the gasps and background sounds my dad took me to the side and said, "Look you can't do this. Listen to me you have to marry her. All of these people are out here. If something goes wrong I will take care of it, but for now, you have to marry her." So to please my father, I married her.

One thing that always stuck with me was regardless of what someone tells you, you must never feel pressured to do anything that you are not committed to do on the inside of your heart. You live inside out, not outside in. The true person you really are is on the inside of you, it's in your heart.

My next memory was my departure day. I was leaving from New Jersey and on a plane heading for basic training in Oklahoma. This happened to be my first time flying what an experience. So, I landed in Lawton, Oklahoma and the air was hot, the sun was bright, and all I felt blowing on me was dry humidity, no wind. The welcome committee was not what others may have thought. There were no special banners, signs, or balloons—just the drill sergeant.

The drive from the airport to the barracks was no joke! The new recruits or soldiers as we were called sat in the back of a cattle truck heading to our new base. When we arrived I remember hearing the brakes stop and then the doors being opened by the drill sergeants screaming and yelling, "Get off the truck, get out NOW!" "You are now in basic training".

With the unexpected screaming and yelling, the other soldiers and I had no clue. All of us hurried off the cattle truck. We were falling and tripping over one another and each other's green duffle bags.

Once we all managed to get off the cattle truck and fall into position as the drill sergeants told us to do, I recall them still screaming and yelling "Get down into the push-up position". *In my mind, I'm thinking but definitely not speaking out loud, "stay calm ... just stay calm" is what I was saying to encourage myself.*

So I am on the ground in the push-up position and being visited face to face with the drill sergeant— uncomfortable to say the least. As I am trying to stay focused in the same timing, I was confronted by the Drill Sergeant. "Oh brother, here we go"

Drill Sergeant: "Where are you from?"

Gerald: "**New Jersey**"–as I screamed

back with toughness in my voice.

Drill Sergeant: "Oh, you think you are tough city Boy?"

Gerald: "**No Drill Sergeant**"–as I looked at him but still wanted him to feel respected.

Drill Sergeant: "Just for that, give me 50 more push-ups."

Gerald: **As my arms were shaking and trembling, I toughed it out and gave him another 50 push-ups."**

I said to myself, if I could make it back on the streets in my hometown, I knew I had to use that same toughness here in Oklahoma. This was going to be a long twelve weeks and today was just the beginning.

Chapter 8

BASIC TRAINING

Starting basic training was rough that first week. The first day was a shocker and an eye opener. After getting settled into my barracks, I was thinking about my hometown, missing it, and this place was far from it! I quickly adjusted and adapted to the military routine of things such as time, exercise, and eating schedules. Back in the New Jersey I would do my own thing when it came to these daily tasks. I guess since I was now governed by the military my mindset had to be according to their schedule.

The daily routine was a 4:30 AM roll call by the drill sergeant who would come in yelling, "Get on your feet, soldiers!". Stumbling out of our bunks trying to stand at attention, the soldiers and I were shaking and trembling through our sleeping eyes. The drill sergeant was rambling out the list of commands for the day. I recalled him ordering others for this and that but I heard him loud and clear when he gave orders for me to be his 'house mouse'. A 'House Mouse' I was thinking, what is this all about? I asked the drill sergeant what was a House Mouse. He defined a House Mouse as: 'A person who takes responsibility for all things in the barracks at all times'. Ok, I think to myself, now I am ready for the challenge.

Challenge that it was, I remember the exercise routines, going on two mile runs, singing military songs as we ran and carried flashlights in our hands since it was dark outside. That brings to mind an example of being a Christian that is a light in a dark place. The dark place would be the world system and the light would be the Christian who has Christ in them, according to Ephesians 5 verse 8.

As far as the eating schedules we all were in the mess hall at 5:30 AM after showering and shaving. After those morning runs and being refreshed by the shower it was a good feeling going thru the lines to get our grub on. The meals we had were good. I recall the time when I got my food along with another buddy and I was scolded because I was talking and given ten seconds to eat and get out of the mess hall. I learned rather quickly that talking and eating was not acceptable here in basic training.

Further along in the later part of basic training the routine became pretty basic. I was being built up and growing in my understanding of how to do things the right way. I was becoming a stronger and better man in life, just as my father told me I would. He also said that the military would make a man out of me and these weeks of basic training was doing just that. I was happy, energized and in shape.

However, I also felt like I was still missing something. That something was my hometown. Despite being here in basic training, I still wanted to know what was going on in the streets. I was glad that we had a furlough coming up and that would get me a week back home. With all of this going on I needed a five day break.

CHAPTER 9

FURLOUGH GOING HOME

*Y*es! I sighed with relief when my name was called for my first furlough. Front and center I was standing eagerly with anticipation for my release to go home. My first visit back to my hometown since being in basic training was finally here!

I was ready. I went back to my barracks, packed my bags and was heading to the bank to cash my check. The only thing left was getting my round-trip ticket and catch the first thing smoking out of Oklahoma. As I was flying on the plane, I was thinking about my life in my hometown. I was going back home to my old lady and to meet my baby girl. I knew she was gorgeous, getting big and missing her daddy. In addition to seeing my mother, father, and brothers just being back in the hood was a relief from basic training.

So as the plane descended I was anticipating what things would look like. I had been gone for over ninety days. I gathered my bags from the baggage area and met my father and we embraced and he said, "Wow man, you got big!" I said, "Yeah, I know, all those push-ups they were making us do." My father said, "Oh don't worry, it's making a man out of you." as we both smiled and laughed walking out towards the car. It was great seeing my father again. I loved him and he had such a good heart.

On the drive home from the airport my father was sharing some personal things with me, which he heard about my old lady. My father gave his words of wisdom as far as never being hen-pecked for a woman. A tough pill to swallow, I still cried a little tear and looked at my father. He said, "I know my son, I have been there before, and I have been hurt by a woman too." Deep inside of my own thoughts, I believed that it's ok to cry…. men do cry.

Just as we began to get a little closer to town I was instantly brought back to the time the drill sergeant would always tell one of the soldiers that Jodie has got your girlie and has gone. Man, I was angry! "Ok" my father says as we were back at the house. My mother came to greet me with a hug.

During the prior moment I was observing on how things looked at the house as we pulled up. My hometown was still looking the same, nothing changed but the buildings. Some were torn down and others were being built up.

Soon, my mother and I are embracing, hugging and holding me ... she is looking me over and saying "how big I got and how much weight I gained." I told her, "Yeah, it's all those push-ups." We both laughed. After the family all gathered around, it was good to be home I thought. Needless to say, I wanted to see my old lady and baby girl. So I called her to come over and she brought the baby. My expression when I saw my child was pure joy! I was so happy.

My old lady and I spoke during this time and were catching up and still something with her didn't feel right in my heart. In the back of my mind, I was thinking about what my father told me in the car. Could all of what he said be true? No, I was thinking, not my old lady.

During this time my brother came in the house and was excited to see me back home and gave me a five and said, "What's up man?" I said to him that I was in the army and things are going well. He said, "Oh yeah, I am getting paid ... I'm getting crazy money and my pockets got the mumps. So I am not messing with the government like that." We all laughed and shook our heads. Then I said "That's my brother money making AD."

What a day and what will tomorrow bring . . . .

Chapter 10

DA HOME-BOYS

With the family settling down for the evening and I also wanted to get a little shut eye. I was quickly reminded of how programmed I really was with the Army. I believed that I was the drill sergeant that morning when I alarmed everyone with my early 4:30 AM wake up call.

In that particular moment, I had instant flash backs from basic training and my father quickly reminded me that I was at home in my hometown and not in Oklahoma! In my sleep walking dazed moment, my father sat up and was talking with me. After he help settled me down and I regained my bearings, I went back to bed and got some sleep.

I was awakened by my mother cooking breakfast in the kitchen and I instantly knew that it was good to be home. During breakfast, my father and mother and I sat down and ate. We talked about how I was doing and they encouraged me by saying it was a good thing for me and to continue staying in the Army. For the first time in a very long time, I felt good by receiving loving words and positive support from both of my parents.

After breakfast was over, it was like instant front page news! I was back in town. Word got around fast and then came the friends ... my homies BB and Al came and we just chilled out on the back patio. They were giving me the 411, about what was going on in the streets. They both shared with me the same information that my father shared about my old lady. As I was listening, I was getting heated by what they were telling me, especially when they said there was some dipping going on behind my back. Needless to say, I knew in my heart it was true. But like they say in the hood, no man wants to get played out by a chick. That is not a good look! So that part of the conversation was squashed, only for me to ask her questions later.

BB and Al were flowing on how much paper my family was getting and how they had the block sold-up. And the beefs that were popping off and what street locations belong to uptown verses downtown and of course who had the freshest rides; Mercedes, Jeeps, Volvo, BMW and Jags. I was saying, Man, all this was going on in the last past ninety days?" Instantly, and in unison, they both were like "Yeah Man". We all laughed.

We just sat around and reminisced about the good old days. BB and Al said that they would get up with me later, that they were heading to the block. So we pounded out and I went towards the phone. Heated, but I wanted answers, and right now!

Within what seemed like five minutes, although it was really fifteen, my old lady was knocking on the front door. She knew what was going on and I was keeping a step ahead. I wanted to make her sweat a little. So we chatted. Then I went straight to the point. I asked her, "When I was away in basic training, was you fooling around on me?"

She told me no! That she wasn't fooling around on me! She also said that she knows who told me that stuff; my brothers, BB and Al! "They get on my so and so nerves, because they always trying to break somebody up! They don't have anybody and nobody wants them!"

While she was yelling and getting her point across, I waved her off and just walked away. I said to her from the distance that I know in my heart that she probably did something and it was over! GET OUT! As she was crying and leaving all at the same time; I too was crying, but still I was trying to be tough.

I got myself together and then made some phone calls to let my homies know that I was coming to meet up with them on the block. As I was going out to meet them, I was riding in my car going over all of this commotion and needed a drink.

Zipped and dipped along with my knocking system that was pumping in my ride, I pulled up and said, "Yo, let's go to the Elks and get a drink". They hopped in and we were off for a much needed cold one.

Chapter 11

THE GLAMOROUS NIGHT

We were all laughing as we headed inside the Elks. The scenery is just like I once remember, music playing, seeing old faces from around the way, women looking tight, laced up from head to toe, the fellas getting their groove on. Man I was excited to be back home in my familiar surroundings. We settled down and copped us a seat. While we were throwing some drinks down, in walks my brother AD. Looking glamorous like he was known for, he was fresh in the cut. AD could put it on. His grey leather short waist coat had white fur around the collar. The belt that was attached was banging. His Cadillac gold medallion necklace was encrusted with diamonds and the weight of his gold necklace was heavy. To top that off, he had his grey leather Bally's to match along with a black hat with a feather in it.

When he made eye contact with us he smirked and smiled. I said, "Man that's bad, where you copped that from, Brooklyn?" As the ladies were coming on to him, on his left and right he said, "Yeah man, something like that" and we both laughed and gave each other high fives as he went on to do his thing. While the crowd in the Elks was giving him his props by saying and chanting, "What's up, Money Making AD?" I headed back to sit down and as I looked around, I saw how the people were drawn to him. AD commanded attention. I was reminded about the movie the "Mack" and I simply smiled and laughed.

After BB, Al and I finished getting our drinks on, we went over to where AD was sitting and chatted up a little bit. We all kicked it, remembering past times, and going back and forth putting blame on one another in a joking manner. It was good just to chill with my brother and homies for a minute. The crowd was still in full force but as time starting passing; it was getting a little late. BB said that he wanted to get some food from the diner. So Al, BB and I told AD that we would get up with him later and we all high fived each other as we left out. When heading out to the car, I noticed that something was different that night. Usually, back in the day at any given moment, a fight would sure enough break out. But with my brother AD inside the

Elks, that was the last thing that was going to happen. One sure thing is that wherever AD went, he held it down, and he had people shook!

As we approached our car, we turned back and looked at the Elks and we see AD coming out with four women which none of these was girlfriend. "What a Mack," we said.

We noticed and heard some random guy apologizing to AD for leaning on his Money Green Cadillac Eldorado car. This guy was saying, "I'm sorry Mr. Money Making AD," as he wiped off the area where he was leaning. Me and the fellas laughed and were like 'wow', as we got in the car and drove away. Inside of the car one of the fellas began to share a story of how AD had the boys in blue shook. When you heard the name AD it rang bells. Everyone knew and knows that he is no joke.

So as we were heading on over to get our grub on, BB made some calls to some young ladies and told them to meet us at the diner. We rolled in, grabbed a booth, and in come the ladies. We laughed at each other because we all had this hidden lingo which was "The 3 F's"–Fool them, Freak them, and Forget them. These chicken heads are dumb! They are so caught up, that the 3 F's are so simple, that it won't faze them. Yeah, it's going to be a glamorous night.

CHAPTER 12

SAYING OUR GOOD-BYES

A new day has dawned and I am feeling like a new man. I had a good time last night chilling out with BB and Al. But now my furlough is up and I have to get packed and ready to head out of New Jersey at 1900 hours. My mom and father left me a note on my dresser saying that old girl called last night. Man I don't even want to go there, not right now. I'll deal with that later. I know they want the best for us but and I want the best also. A knock at my bedroom door—oh man, who is it? I was saying to myself and praying at the same time, I hope it is not my old lady? "Yeah," I say.

The response is my father voice asking to come in to talk to me. "Sure," I said. So my father proceeds to come in and says it's time for us to have a father and son talk. We both sit down on my bed and he tells me that I can't hold onto grudges and that I have to forgive and let things go.

He told me that holding onto bad feelings is not the way to handle the situation and that if for some reason things do not work out, he would take full responsibility for them. I said, Dad, I know what you mean and I am going to hold you at your word. I told you that I didn't want to marry her but you told me to do the right thing. So I am going to do the right thing, and work it out with her."

My father was relieved as he began to share with me that he did not want me to make the same mistakes that he made with my mother. I said, "Thanks for the real heart to heart talk." He said, "I know son. I know son. I have been there too." We hugged and said we loved each other. That was just a real father to son talk.

As my father walked out, I heard my mom telling him to get me to pick up the phone, that I had a call. He looked at me and we both knew who was on the phone. I sighed and he said, "You will be ok son." "I know, dad," I said. I shut my door and picked up the phone and it was my old lady. We talked and she shared with me some things that were really going on and I shared what I felt about them with her. She asked where we stood in our relationship. I told her that we could work things out but not to reminisce on past things. She was excited; I could hear it in her voice.

I told her that we had to stop hurting one another because two wrongs don't make a right. Silently, I was really speaking out loud only to clear my conscience about the "3 F's" from last night. We said that we loved each other, and I told her what time she and the baby should be ready to leave. We were going to start a new life together in a new place and a different environment. As we hung up, I felt better because I understood what my father was saying and truly wanted a fresh start.

The mid-morning was progressing as my brothers and other family came by to see me off. They gave me reassurance about getting out of my hometown and staying positive and that the ARMY is a great step for me. I was thankful that they showed how much they cared. My mother and father were still entertaining as I slipped out to go and get my old lady and baby girl. We were leaving in a couple of hours and I still wanted to see my brother AD and some other peeps on the block.

After picking up my old lady and baby, we swung by the block to check out my peeps and to see where AD was at. I saw just about everyone that evening and asked where he was. They told me he was down on Macy's Boulevard. So we headed on over to Macy's and there here was, getting paper, hustling in his ARMY getup fatigues, timberlands, and his skullcap. I got out the car and gave him a high five and asked, "You planning on going Army, dressed like that?" and he responded, "Nah man, you in that ARMY!" and high fived me back. He asked me to walk with him to his car, we both got in and sat and talked for a minute.

He said, "I see you and your old lady are back together and I guess you taking her back with you?" I told him yeah and he said, "Ok man, if that's what you want, I can't stop you from what you want to do, just be careful because I don't want her to play you out like a sucka." I said, "Ok man, we're good."

As he opened up the glove compartment he had like about thirty thousand dollars of cash in there. I asked him "Man you getting money like this." He said "Yeah man." I would never tell him but looking at all that cash, made me nervous. Before we left out the car he said to me "I have money, I have women, I have cars and gold but something is still missing, there has to be another way out."

That conversation with AD opened my eyes because, he was telling me in some form of another, at the age of eighteen, when a teenager desires so much freedom and peace, he didn't have it even with all his money, his women and his cars.

But in his heart he knew there was something much deeper, and a better way. In hind sight, now that I am a born again believer of Jesus Christ, those words that AD spoke remind me of the scripture <u>of John 14,</u>

Verse 6: When Jesus said, *I am the way, the truth and the life and no man gets to the father but by me.* Jesus is the way and that word way means a direction, wow. Putting it simply, my brother AD was searching for a way to go. He knew that all of his money, cars, women, and gold were not the true answer. The truth is Jesus! He was missing a peace only Jesus can give.

As AD and I left out of his car, I shook his hand and we gave each other a hug. Needless to say that same hug was the very last one that AD and I shared together. Within one month time after me and my old lady and my baby girl returned to my new base in Georgia, I got a phone call that there was a turf war going on and that Money Making AD was MURDERED! The top of his head and left side of his face was blown off by a sawed-off shot gun and his body was dumped on a dead end street. When they found him he was lying face up and his face was covered in blood. His bullet proof vest could not protect him nor stop that shot gun blast. After hearing this, I cried and left and the phone dangling...

The greatest tragedy in life is not death. It is an unfulfilled purpose! In John 10:10 the enemy come to steal, kill and destroy. Jesus said, *"I come that you might have life and have it more abundantly."* But it really is about the choices and decisions we can make.

CHAPTER 13

THE CHAOS

I was vexed and was going to take matters into my own hands. My brother AD's death was not going to be taken in vain. Something was going to be done! I knew who that someone was, me and my other brothers. Vengeance was going to be ours. And the streets that AD left behind were going to be ours, too. I just had to get through his funeral, and boy, was it a fashion show. There were about 300 people of men and women that I could remember who were in furs, minks, gold and were dressed to impress. The others that came to show their love were dressed clean as well they were dressed up in suits with leather jackets and some of the hottest sneakers, too. As the fashion scenery was beyond words, I on the other hand, was working up a plan in my mind so my brothers and I could hold down the same areas that AD maintained.

As far as the ARMY making a good solider out of me, they could forget it. I had no plans on returning. Especially since, I am back here in New Jersey. My old lady and my relationship had come to that ultimate stressing point! I had no care in the world! I was blaming and telling her that AD was right when he told me to leave her alone. AD was gone and I was in another state when it all went down. I knew that streets were hot with the 411, but no one was talking yet. The cops and city officials were in fear of retaliation.

While my brothers and were working on the perfect master plan, my mother's and father's prayers were that they didn't want to see any more of their children dead! My mother also took a bold stand and was speaking up in the local newspapers about ending gangs and their turf wars. More than ever there was a stronger presence of cop cars on patrol in the hood. People from uptown were representing and showing more respect for Money Making AD by wearing the Army Fatigues and Boots.

Although the streets lost a good solider, AD's presence was still there. My whole mindset was now about how my brothers and I were going to get the paper like AD. We had more reason than ever! The ones who took his life had no care and neither did we. Like Money

Making AD used to always say, "Hard to the Head, No Punking Out." It was on.

I was picking up the mantle that AD left behind. I now had the money, the women and plenty of cars. I remember all of my cars. I had a Navy Blue Mustang Convertible 5.0 with some banging Dayton's. A Jaguar two door coupe SJS, the color was money green and had beige leather interior and sat on twelve cylinders. My Jeep was a mad hot aqua green, hammer rims, a knocking system with a grey leather ragtop. I had stashed mad paper in the speakers and rims. I was doing it like that on the streets. I had a cocky attitude, my head was puffed up. I was conceited and a cheater. I was never faithful to the women I had both locally and out of state. When I would go out to the clubs, I would tell the women that I loved them knowing that I was lying because I did not know what love was. I thought I had an idea of what love was, but it was just simple lust.

When I would take the women shopping, I would treat them to the finer things in life. When these women were on my arm they always rocked. With Fendi, Louie Vuitton, and Gucci I kept them looking sharp. Not forgetting the accessories, they were laced in jewelry, handbags, and high-heels. It was nothing for us to head over to NYC for shopping sprees. But the glitz and gam would back fire on me when I would have hotel run-ins.

I would select which woman I wanted to be with and if I chose someone different then what their expectation was, somehow they would find out the hotel location. Man, did I suffer the consequences! My windows were busted out with baseball bats. My tires were slashed, and my car had endless scratches from the key marks. Despite all of the paper I was getting on the streets, I never thought that my out of pocket expenses would be on the regular like this, with all that car repairing. Something had to give, this was getting old!

From the women fighting at the clubs, in streets, and around the hood, they never stopped for one moment to look to see who the new lady was that I had riding in my car with me! I guess they were catching up from last week when they saw the other one in their spot and duke it out. Wow is all I could say. Sad but true.

But when your name is Jay Bond 007, in the end, it only makes you wonder who the women really wanted—me or my paper!

Despite how much I had it going on in the streets I still did not have a peace with all of those material things, my cars, money, women, and clothes. I am not saying that God does not want you to have nice things. He does want you to have nice things, but God does not want those nice things to control of you. God truly wants to be first in your life. He wants nothing before him. For if you put anything before him, those things will become your God. The above describes the definition of idolatry.

Exodus 20:4-6 – reads: *Thou shall not make unto thee any graven images or any likeness of anything that is heaven above, or that is in the earth beneath, or that is in the water under the earth; thou shall not bow thyself to them, nor serve them for I the Lord thy God am a jealous God, visiting inequity of the fathers upon the children unto the third and fourth generation of them that hate me. And showing mercy unto thousands of them that love me and keep my commandments.*

WHAT HAPPENS NEXT IN THE HOOD

WILL ANYTHING GOOD COME
OUT OF IT?

*A*s you have just read <u>From Hood to Good Part 1</u>, I am sure you are left wondering what happens next! It is amazing how God completely changed my life. I went from family hardships, life disappointments, the passing of my real father, women drama, accepting AD's death, turf battles in my hood, and trying to get my younger brother to turn away from the gang before he was the next one to be killed or put in jail. Well, God did spare his life although he was not killed but he is now serving over one hundred years in state prison. Like myself as well, my brother has accepted Jesus Christ as his personal savior and redeemer.

The sequel and much anticipated follow-up book <u>From Hood to Good Part 2</u> shares so much internal reflection and much needed truth that everyone who reads and can experience some of these same life trials themselves. We all have a purpose and gift that is placed inside of us. God is the source of the purpose you have, and when asked, he will reveal it to you.

Hind sight is always twenty-twenty as the ole folks would say. What I know now, after experiencing this type of lifestyle is that there is an enemy out there that is real and is the master of deception and destruction. My opening my heart and sharing with you as the reader what I have gone through it is an attempt to cancel the assignment of further deception and destruction from the enemy. I have been blessed to grow more in the grace of God. After God changed my life around, I have continued to give him all the Glory for what he has done in and through me. **Remember this scripture and keep in your heart.** *For it is God which worketh in you both to will and do of his good pleasure* – Philippians 2:13.

From Hood to Good Part 2 is an eye opener and life changer. Believe me when I tell you will not be disappointed with this book at all! I thank you in advance and look forward to sharing my life experiences From Hood to Good Part 2 with you.

From Hood to Good Part 2 coming soon!

Hello my fellow readers!

Get ready, get ready, here comes the highly anticipated From Hood to Good Part II; life journey experiences. Family life struggles, trials, tragedy, triumphs, celebrations and even great victories!

CHAPTER 1

The family

*A*fter my brother was killed, I suffered mentally. So I started getting heavy back in the game; getting paper! I also went AWOL from the Army after what happened to A.D. I have to keep it real, or keep it one hundred, I was stressed out! I didn't know which way to turn or who to turn to. So me and my homeys started hustling and getting women. You know, trying to be a player! To be honest, the clubs used to be off the chain! People shooting up the place and fighting like cats and dogs. That was crazy. Now, I look back over my life and I say, I could've been killed out there in those streets! It was only the grace of God that kept me alive. God is good!

So, now I'm back in my hometown me and my homeboys at the park chilling and pumping our music. Girls were on our jocks because we were out there getting all that paper. Paper was coming fast, lots of it in a major way. I told my homeboys that after we had clocked out we were going back to NYC to cop more products. My homeboys, with no hesitation, said, "No doubt!" I told them that we are getting paid and they just started laughing. We were serious about that paper. So we left the park and started to head back to NYC. We said that we are getting paid in full and our pockets got the mumps and nobody could stop us! We are unstoppable.

So we went to the city and we picked up our products. On our way going back home, we crossed the bridge and came to the toll booth to enter the turnpike. As we were riding, the boys in blue starting following us and I was like, "oh no, this can't be happening!" So my homeboy panicked and tossed the product out of the car window. Then came the signals and the sirens were flashing bright. I was like we are hit. The boys in blue pulled us over, quickly asked for our license and registration. They started checking the car and didn't find the product at first and then they said, "don't move, freeze." One of the authorities told us that they saw someone toss something out of the window and they actually went back and found it. Indeed, we got incarcerated! But, one thing I learned is that the boys in blue is not against you, they are against crime. You know that saying, "don't do the crime if you can't do the time." LOL!

They took me to the adult facility, the county. It was one of the roughest camps in NJ. They were known for beating people for their fly sneakers and taking their food. I was like, "man I'm not giving nothing up in here." Huh, I guess I have to fight! I went to the dorms where people were locked up. It was like the wild, wild west in the facility! People were playing cards and gambling, it was just like the streets. The tv was on and they were watching it, some were working out lifting weights. On the other hand, my homey was younger than me and he was taken to juvenile corrections and his charges were dropped. They let him go. I went with the big boys in the facility. It was a whole lot different. While I'm in jail, I quickly got on the phone and called my father and asked him for bail money. Guess what happened? He said, "Sorry, I don't have the money." I was devastated and said, "What? Are you kidding me?" He said, "what about your jewelry, nice tims and your gold chains and your fly cars, (laughing). I guess he was teaching me a lesson. So eventually I made bail and got out. But this was crazy, because when I made bail, the MP's were waiting on me to come out so they could escort me to the stockade. Wow, I made bail to get out of jail, then I ended up back in jail by the MP's. That was wild. So the boys in blue took me to court in a couple of days and they asked me why did I go AWOL. I told them that I was under a lot of stress because of what had happened to my brother A.D. when he got killed. God had to have been with me because they gave me so much pity and let me go with a program and a little guard duty. Wow, God's hand was on my life and I didn't even know it.

Finally, I came home and saw my mother and father and family and they were happy to see me. I was tripping when I got home. I said to myself, never again! That place was crazy. Booth visits, no touching and people out in the world will leave you for dead. It was so true what you sow, is what you reap. Galatians 6:7.

Mom and dad (respectfully called GT), got back together after seventeen years of separation. Who would've thought they'd get together again. I admit that I was happy about it. They had my little brother and he is now in his late twenties and is married with a child of his own and works a 9-5 job. He also has a relationship with God.

I was so used to being raised by my step-father and living by what he taught me that listening to my dad became irritating. My real father didn't know me and once he tried to beat me with a belt when I was fifteen. I told him that I was too old for a beating and that it was too late. Lol! I didn't understand the lesson he was trying to teach me. He told me that I needed to go to the military so that they could make a man out of me.

Thinking back today, my dad taught me valuable lessons because the military did give me discipline.

My father was an awesome businessman. He received his degree in Business from a very well-known prestigious University. He was a salesman at heart and he told me that America was like a big supermarket; as long as you have something to sell, you will always be productive. He owned a couple of Cadillac's and two homes, which back then was status! He showed me so many things about life in the short period of time that I knew him. A few weeks after I got home, I received some very disturbing news about my dad. He wasn't doing well. I was shocked and floored. My father whom I loved and had just had met, was going to die. I said to myself, this can't be happening. I just lost my brother a year ago and now my father. Stunned and shocked, not a word to say but a tear rolled down my cheek. He was so young, only 41, diagnosed with pancreatic cancer. I went through a very hard time after he died. He did not leave me any material possessions when he passed away, because he knew that if I got that money, I would have probably gone bonkers with all that dough! My father was wise and left me great words of wisdom and some good nuggets to chew on. The bible says that "wisdom is the principle thing, therefore get wisdom; in all thy getting, get understanding".

~Proverbs 4:7.

Wisdom produces money, but money doesn't produce wisdom.

I was hurting from my dad's passing so I went looking for love on the streets. I got back into the game hard! The boys in "blue" knew me well. I had money, cars, women, jewelry, etc. Life was getting rough though, because sin is a hard life to live.

They way of a transgressor is hard.

~Proverbs: 15:23.

CHAPTER 2

New Beginnings, the Mid-west was a mess!

I had to raise my daughter because by then her mother and I had parted ways. My mother did most of the raising and she did an awesome job. I thank God for my mother! I always spent money on my daughter but never enough time with her. All I did was focus on the streets. Knowing that hanging out there on the streets was heading on the path of destruction. The streets had me! Money became my God!

I started another relationship with a fly red-bone. We had daughters and lived in the hood (From Hood to Good, come on somebody), and we were living the "good life", or so it seemed. Money was no object so I took her on shopping sprees in NYC a lot. We were like Bonnie and Clyde back then. I was out there getting paper and she was spending it! She had my back though.

My daughters were dressed well. They had Polo leather jackets and shearling coats all straight from New York from Delancey Street. Nothing was too good for them I thought. Even though I was living that life, I started worrying that the boys in blue would raid the house. I had NO peace! Something was missing as I struggled with fear.

Since money making A.D. was a kingpin, being his brother opened a lot of doors for me on the streets. I became well known as J Bond. I was flashy and cocky and five-o were on me. Things were getting heated out there, so my old lady thought that we should move away for a couple of years. She told me she had family in the mid-west and thought we should move out there with them. By now, I was in fear and chaos was all around me. It was getting too hot out there living that life! So, we went to the mid-west! We took a bus from New York; children, suitcase and all. It took thirty-six hours to get there!

I met her family and it was really difficult because I had to learn to get a job. That wasn't easy. I was so used to getting what I wanted and making endless money that I didn't know how to adapt to the change. It was hard trying to be a family man and do it with a regular 9-5. Sometimes it got to me and brought me to an ultimate stressing point.

We both started working and eventually got our own apartment and car. It was different; no one was looking for me. It was a change of pace and a very different lifestyle to get used to. As the weeks went by, I checked out the city and we both started going to the clubs. I met a guy named Chuck in a fast food joint. He told me that they were clocking dollars there too! We connected.

We hooked up and put a plan together then started making paper. More than I ever did before! Wow, how things change when you go to a different state! Chuck met my girl and she said that I should watch the company I keep and reminded me that we were trying to have a better life. I didn't pay her any mind, I was back on top! But the Word of God says "bad company corrupts good character."

~I Corinthians 15:33.

Chuck and I started doing our thing on the streets, he showed me around town. He was intrigued that I came from out of state, so he wanted to know about the hats and clothes that I was rocking. So we decided that we would go to NYC soon so he could get some gear. He wanted to get a shearling coat for his daughter too. We gave each other some dap and smiled, it was on! My girl said that it seemed that we were doing the same stuff like back home and nothing was changing so she was constantly on me. Not knowing what I know

now as I am a born-again believer, the only way you can change is getting your mind renewed to the word of God continually, which is a day to day process. I kept doing the same thing over and over getting no results. When you keep doing the same thing and you are getting no results, this is called the spirit of insanity!

While still in the mid-west, I met one of Chuck's friends and his name was KG. KG had a girlfriend and they were out there balling too! So we all hooked up, started hanging out at the clubs and getting to know each other. Come to find out, KG was the Big man out there in the Midwest getting paper! As we got deeper in the game, come to find out he had beefs with other people out of state over territory. KG was a big dude, he had his weight up and people feared him! He and his girl had issues and some major problems and Chuck knew about them. KG and I would sometimes be by our self and he would be stressing saying that he and his girl were having problems. He said he had no peace or happiness. I would talk to him and tell him to stay focused and not to let stuff get to him. He said "I love her and I told him, I hear you man, I hear you". Chuck and I talked and we both knew that every time KG went out of state, his girl was messing around on the DL. After that, KG must've sensed it in his heart, because he felt that something wasn't right. They were already having problems.

About a week later I saw KG at the corner store, he said, "what up J Bond, how do you like it here?" I said, "It's a slower pace, it's cool, it's different than being up north." Then he said, "That's good, what are you doing right now, you got time to take me somewhere?" Nothing, just getting something to drink, I'll be right out. I came out the store, he gave me dap and we got into my whip. It was an Audi, I bought an Audi as soon as I got to the mid-west, I paid cash for it. He asked me to drive and we were bopping our heads to the music listening to one of the dope rap songs that were out at the time.

As we were driving, he started talking about his girl, telling me about what they were going through. I told him that it was going to be alright. He asked me to take him to get some roses for her. I thought to myself, wow, he must really be in love with her. Come to find out roses have an affinity with women and it acts as a mild sedative and anti-depressant which uplifts the spirits. We stopped and got some red roses and a couple of teddy bears too. We got back into the whip; he had a smile on his face. He asked me to take him by her house hoping to make things better between them. We got to her house, he knocked on the door to give her the roses, but she wasn't there, so he gives them to her mother, she told him that they were beautiful and that she would give them to her. KG came back to the car and he said I hope she likes them and I told him that she would love them. He smiled. I was just giving him encouragement, that's what friends are for. It's amazing that like in the bible, it says that we should encourage one another. That's what I was doing.

He said, "Could you drop me off over by the projects so that I could take care of some business?" I told him, no problem. I dropped him off and I went back home to spend time with my family. I talked to my girl and she asked me where I had been, and I told her that I was taking care of business. She said to me that she hoped that it was productive business. The next day, I went to work for a temp agency for a shoe warehouse and it was a blessing in disguise. Later during the week, I ran into BB. He was shaking his head, and I asked him what was wrong. He told me that I would never believe what happened. He told me that KG had been shot several times, he was murdered. It is amazing how when you are out there doing things in the streets that you think you have it going on. It is a set up by the enemy and it is also a path of destruction. The bible says, "There is a way that seems right to a man but the end is the way of destruction."

~Proverbs 14:12

Also, in John 10:10, the word of God says the enemy comes to steal, kill and destroy, but Jesus came to give life and life more abundantly! Hallelujah!

So word got out about what happened to KG and my girl found out and she said that it was crazy that this happens everywhere we go. I told her that she was right. She said she couldn't take this mess and that I was doing same old thing that I did before. After that, I talked to my man BB and I told him that it was crazy and that I would still work my regular 9-5 and continue to be on the low. After about a month went by, I was working and taking care of my family, I talked to my girl and we started making plans. We had a conversation and she didn't see any changes and she didn't want to live in fear, and she said she really didn't like it there, so we decided to go back home. Up North it was!

We got the children packed, suitcase and all so we could go back to New Jersey. Before I headed back, I contacted Chuckto let him know I was headed back up north. He said, "Man you leaving?" I told him, "Yeah man I'm bouncing, I'm going back up top man. My girl and I had an agreement that we would go back home. Things weren't working out like we planned it. He said, "Ok, let's stay in touch." So we exchanged numbers and he gave me some dap and we smiled. I said to myself, "It's amazing how you have your own things planned out and it doesn't work, but when I see things now as a born again believer, how God clearly states in Jeremiah 29:11; for I know the plans I have for you, declares the Lord, plans to prosper you, plans to give you hope and a future." God's plan DOES work!

CHAPTER 3

Back up North!

*A*s I go back up north with my girl and my family, while we were looking for a place to stay, we stayed with her mother uptown. Again, after I got settled, I saw my homeboys and they said "hey J Bond, how you been doing man, It's been a long time since we seen you. What you been up to? A lot of things have changed since you been gone." I told them that I've been gone for a couple of years out of state

Yeah, but now I'm back. They told me that was good. I went to check on my family. My mother and my brothers were doing well and they were happy to see me. I asked my mom what was going on and she told me that it was the same old thing nothing had changed. After several weeks passed, I started the same thing over again, back in the streets getting paper. Within about a month's time I went to the car dealership with my brother and bought a 5.0 drop top Mustang convertible with Dayton's on it. It was fast! Paid straight I cash for it, no car note for me!

We drove into the city with the drop top down with the music pumping the girls were jocking, my homeboys on the corner were clocking. We pulled over and we stopped on our block and people were saying that they liked my whip and they asked me how much I paid for my car and I said "a lil' something, something." They laughed and gave me dap. They said, "I hear you man, it reminds me of the car in the movie that came out in the 1990's. As weeks go by, I get a call from my man Chuck. He asked me what I was up to and I told him just shucking and jiving man, making things happen. There are three types of people in the world today, people who make things happen, people who wonder what happened, and people who watch things happen. If you want anything in life, you gotta make it happen!!

Chuck responded and told me he heard me. He said, "Well, for me man out here it's a lot of slow motion, so I'm coming out there with you to make things happen." I told him, "ok bet, let me know when you gonna come." He said, I'll be there next week." I said, "Ok." So it was on, Chuck was on his way up north!

After he came up north, I met him at the bus station and we talked and got a bite to eat at a fast food joint.

Chuck said he liked it up north, he said it was a gold mine and the weather was nice, it was the fall season. We sat down and started getting our plans together about how to we were going to do things. I asked him how the bus ride was and he told me it was decent, he slept through most of it. After we finished eating, we carried his bags through the bus terminal; we headed to the car and loaded his bags. It was on! Chuck and I were on our way to my house to get settled. After we arrived, he wanted to take a shower and get freshed up. When he was done, he wanted me to show him around. We went out and he met a couple of my homeboys out on the block. He also met some of my family and friends. Chuck said that he liked the city with the tall buildings. He asked me how the clubs in the city were. I told him they were nice and I asked him if he wanted to go and he said yes. I told him that we could go that night at about eleven, that's when the clubs started jumping.

As the night went on, I told old girl that Chuck was in town and I would get up with her later. She said ok, she asked me to let her know when I would be back, (smiling the whole time). As the night progressed Chuck and I went to the crib to get dressed for the club. He pulled out the gators and some nice dress pants and a casual suede jacket, and I told him "man you look sharp, you look so sharp, you probably could cut me up". He said, "man, go head" and laughed. I got dressed and put on a nice casual suit jacket with dress pants and Bally's and we were on our way to the club! As soon as we get there, the women were on us, especially BB because he was from out of town. Fresh meat! We danced on the floor with a couple of females and had some drinks and Chuck met a nice young lady. She was a fly red-bone and her body was banging! Chuck was like, "man I need to get with that, she's feeling me". I told him, "go ahead, I see her looking at you". So he pushed up and it was on! He started talking to her and by the time the club was over, he was going home with her. He told me that he would call me later and that he was going to spend some time with her. Then before he left, he asked me did I know her, and I said "yeah, she is from around the way." He said, "alright, bet, I'll give you a call later." I told him that I would give him a call later to check on him, I was about to bounce too. I went back to the crib to be with my girl, she asked me, "How was it?" I told her it was cool, he met a nice young lady; I think she is some of your people. She was like, "oh, small world huh?" I said yeah.

The next day arrived and at about at eleven am I get a call from Chuck asking me to pick him up at a hotel. I told him I'd be there in about fifteen minutes. I got to the hotel and he got in the car and we drove off and headed to the crib. I asked how his night was and he said that it was good man. I said, "You knocked some boots last night huh?" He started laughing and said, "man go head, man you know how we do, we spin them like a top, fool 'em, freak 'em, and forget 'em."

Chapter 4

Heavy in the game.

*L*ater that week, Chuck and I hooked up. I asked him what he wanted to do. I told him about an amusement park. We went out there, got on some rides and ate some of the foods there. We shot some hoops, talked and had a great time, a blast! They had fireworks at night and it wasn't the 4th of July. We went back to the crib so he could get his things and BB told me that he had to take care of some business back home so he said he would be back. He said, "You know I gotta stick and move man." He told me he had to go down south to take care of some unfinished business. I gave him dap and told me I'd keep in touch. He said ok and told me to stay focused, handle my business and stop putting all of my strength into women. Girls come a dime a dozen, they let you down and break your heart. "I've been there before," he said. One thing that I know about Chuck and I'm a man of God today is that II Corinthians 5:17 is right. It says therefore, if anyone is in Christ, he is a new creation, old things have passed away, behold, all things have become new. Some of the things he said made a lot of sense. I took him to the bus stop and dropped him off in NYC. I gave him a hand shake and told him I'd get up with him later. He said, "ok man, stay in touch."

It's amazing today as I am serving the Lord and in ministry being effective for God's glory. The scripture says the Word is a lamp unto my feet and a light to my path. There is path set before each person, but it depends on what path you're on. Some of us were out there on the path living a life of the world not knowing where that path was going to lead to. Taking a chance just having "fun" in the world sense but not for the kingdom, we're lost with no direction. It was nothing but the grace of God that kept us alive. We messed around with different women we didn't really know, could've caught diseases, but it was by His grace. We risked our lives every day but God had His hand on our lives and we didn't even know it. That's how good God is. In Jeremiah 1:5, God says that before you were formed in your mother's body, He knew you and you had a Holy purpose for your life. Basically, we all existed before we got here. Amen.

As several months go by, I talked to my brothers and cousins; and they asked me if I had heard from Chuck and I told them no, I hadn't talked to him in a while. I found out through the grapevine that he had gotten into some trouble out of state and he was locked up for a crime and was facing a lot of time! I was shocked, confused and startled. I couldn't believe it. His bail was very high! After that happened to Chuck, I thought to myself, man, that's crazy. I have to be careful, he always told me to stay focused. Time passed and I was still out on the streets getting paper in my town. One day the boys in blue had a surprise raid and we didn't know it. They came from every direction and they told us to freeze and lay down. They had on army fatigues and camouflaged pants and I had on a pair too! It's amazing when you're in the world and you know you're doing things wrong. Whatever you sow, you reap! My mother used to always tell me, leave those streets alone, because whatever you sow, you reap. My mother was quoting the bible and the word was always around us, but we never took heed to it. Even our grandmothers prayed for us and told us about Jesus but we never listened. You know the saying, a hard head makes a soft behind.

After the boys in blue raided, they told us to freeze and don't move. They were clapping their hands saying, "We got him." I just put my head down and said, "Man, that's it." I got locked up that day and my bail was one hundred thousand dollars! I'll never forget that day; I saw my life flash before my eyes and I said this is the end. Everything that I did the cars, fun, women, the money and status, my reputation, flashy clothes all came to a screeching halt. It's amazing how when the cops said freeze, my life froze! Literally! I was taken downtown, booked up and sent into population. People saw me and said, "Wow, they finally got J Bond." I had like a ten year run. I thought that I could never get caught. But my time was up!

What was so sad about it that I had children to take care of and I had to leave them with their mother to let her raise them without me. It's a trip sometimes when after things happen, you think about what you could've, would've or should've done. So while I'm in there with a $100,000 bail, I called moms and told her I was locked up. She asked me what was my bail amount, and I told her the amount. She said, "that's not bail, that's ransom!" She asked if I had any money saved up and I told her yes, I'd have to get a lawyer. I told her I'd have to call one of my partners to get this paper so I could make this bail. I was in there for about three weeks to a month and my bail dropped to $75,000 and I made bail and came home. When I got home I chilled for minute and I walked into the store and had my daughters with me. One of the men in blue saw me, jumped out and asked me, "How'd you get out?" I told him I made bail. He didn't believe me at first so he called in to make sure and they confirmed it. He told me alright go on your way man, be careful out there."

CHAPTER 5

Caught and released

$\mathscr{I}$ had hired a lawyer and he took care of my cases and I didn't have to go back until sentencing that following year. I was facing some time but I only had to do three and I came home through a halfway house.

After I did my time a few years went by, I finished my time and I came home, my girl and I had broken up but remained friends. My weight was up. You know how it is when you're in there working out, eating three meals a day and lifting weights. Everybody was like, "J Bond is home." They were like, "he got big too." LOL. Remember, when in my time, money making A.D., J Bond, Nut and Fly by night was known for getting that cheddar and holding the block down as they would say.

While I had been home for a short time, some things went through my mind while I was in there. I wanted to make a change. I got sick and tired of doing the same things over again. It was something in my heart that wanted to make a change. I'm here today to tell you as I am a true believer in Christ Jesus, that God is truly good. When I came home I was determined and had a desire within my heart to want to change. You have to want it! It's like playing football; you have to want to score. You have to want to catch the ball and get the touchdown. You gotta want to get off the bench and get in the game, be a success and be all that God created you to be. You need to know that when God created you, you were fearfully and wonderfully made. You were designed very uniquely, one-of-a-kind and there is no one like you. No one can do what you were born to do. You are talented and gifted and original in the sight of God! You have to remember, only God can change you, not people, not man, not woman, only God can change you-the one that created you!

After I'm home a while, God is so amazing, I met a young lady and started dating her. We hooked up and she heard about my past, but she never let that stop what she saw inside of me. She always told me she saw goodness and greatness inside of me and no one actually ever told me that before. Her words were very encouraging to me; so much that I got a job. After all the things I had been through, when things looked hopeless, I was still able to get a good job. I'm here to tell you today, all things are possible with God. Luke 1:37.

After I started working at my job, I still didn't have it all together. Something was still missing and it was Jesus, but I didn't know that Jesus was the answer back then. So I still kept doing things in my own way. Even with the new job trying to do things the right way, I still got caught up. I began messing with a couple of homeboys and starting doing the same thing again. Getting paper! I tried doing it in a different way this time. Trying to be slick and get over.

I was thinking to myself, I'm out here doing the same thing, in the clubs, women, cheating, not being faithful, telling women I loved them and I was lying because I didn't have a clue what love was. In reality, it wasn't love, it was lust. As I'm living that lifestyle, heading on a path of destruction, the bible says, man's goings are of the Lord, so how can a man understand which way he is going? Basically, if you're not following God, you are lost! The definition of lost is people without God.

I was still with the same young lady and she found out that I was cheating. We weren't getting along because we didn't have anything to stand on. We couldn't stand on anything because we didn't have a foundation with God in it. So then I realized things were changing in my life.

Chapter 6

Salvation…The Greatest Miracle

One day my young lady friend had an appointment at a doctor's office and I met this lady who worked there who was a minister. She told me about Jesus. She said, "Jesus can change your life." I was like, "I don't wanna hear about no Jesus! Jesus can't do nothing for me!" I was thugged out of my mind that day. I had on jeans, tims, my hat to the back and shiny gold teeth. Also, I was dirty at the time (had product on me). I was being ministered to while I had drugs on me. Ain't that something, the Holy Ghost was convicting me! But look at me now. I'm saved, sanctified and filled with the Holy Ghost! Hallelujah! She went on to say, "You need Jesus and you need to get out of the streets before you end up getting killed." I was like wow! This had to be the Spirit of God using her because she didn't even know me. She told me to take her number because I was going to need Jesus. Something told me to take that number and I took it.

Three months later, I was going through some tough times in my life, cheating, arguing with different women and just a life of confusion. I was trying to be a player. I even contemplated suicide at one point. I was driving my car on a Saturday evening and pulled over to the side of the road and I remembered that I had that minister's phone number. I took it out of my wallet and I began to dial the number. When I called the minister woman of God, she answered the phone and I was crying and I said, "That I can't take it no more; the women, the cheating and getting paper. I was sick and tired of being tired, I'm about to take myself out!" She said, "No you're not, Jesus loves you and I'm going to pray for you right now!" She started to pray and it was so powerful that it quickened my spirit. It is so true; the effectual fervent prayer of a righteous man availeth much and is dynamic in His power. James 5:16. So she prayed with me while I was crying on the phone. She told me that she was coming to take me to church tomorrow. It was a Saturday that I'll never forget. I told her ok, I was ready to go to church. It was a powerful sermon with God's word; it was like she was speaking directly to me. I was nervous during the service, thinking about all the things I'd done in my past.

The Pastor preached an anointed sermon based on forgiveness and she said that God had already forgiven me for everything I had done because of His unconditional love, grace and mercy. Also, how Jesus paid the price on the cross.

She had an alter call asking if anyone who wanted to give their life to Christ. I went to the altar and gave my life to Christ sincerely from my heart. I was tired of the streets, living a destructive life with no peace or joy. Those streets were not a joke! Romans 10:9 says if you confess with your mouth that Jesus is Lord and believe in your heart that God raised Jesus from the dead, you shall be saved. For with the heart that one believes unto righteousness, and with the mouth confession is made unto salvation. I want to thank God that I'm saved today and I'm a new creature in Christ Jesus! The bible says, therefore, if any man be in Christ he is a new creation, old things have passed away, all things become new. II Corinthians 5:17.

Wow, God is good! So after I got saved, it was very different for me. It was a process because I never grew up in church. I had to learn who I was I Christ because I didn't know that my Christian walk had to be a lifestyle of faith. According to Romans chapter 1:17, it says that the just shall live by faith! I knew from my old lifestyle how to get that paper on the streets and to go to the clubs and party all night. I had to take some bible courses to find out who King David was and also Absalom and Joshua. I took the classes also for spiritual development and to find out who I was in Christ because it's more than hollering and shouting in church. We need to have our minds renewed to the word of God so that we can know who we are in Christ Jesus and to fulfill our assignment for the Kingdom of God. As I was living my Christian life, people were always trying to pull me back into the game and into the streets and into the world. But I was determined not to go back! God had sent mentors in my life which was a big help in my Christian walk. The bible says iron sharpens iron. That is very important as believers today in the body of Christ. It's good for us to encourage and help one another to let people know that they're not alone. That they have brothers and sisters to help build up their character as a Christian because you can't go anywhere in life without character. I had to do a lot of stuff all over again like obtaining my driver's license. I went from a jag to a cab, from the top of the bottom. From being the man to honoring God who is not a man! Because God is a Spirit, and they that worship Him must worship Him in Spirit and in truth. John 4:24. God was speaking to me now and I had to do things His way and not the enemy's way any longer. Anything Jesus gives you will last, and anything the devil gives you won't last because it's deception and a lie. Romans 3:4 says "let God be true and every man a lie." So the process was on! Doing it God's way and not my way! I had to obtain my driver's license again because I was off the chain! I used to rip up traffic tickets after they gave them to me and I would say, "I ain't paying nothing! I'll pay up when they catch up!" And boy when they caught up, I paid up! I had to pay fines and I had to take the road test all over again. But even in the midst of that, God gave me incredible favor. I failed the road test the first time, but I passed it the second time. That's a testimony to someone who has failed. You can do all things through Christ who strengthens you. Philippians 4:13. God is good, so never give up; If God be for you, who can be against you; Romans 8:31. Remember saints, we have to continue to fight the good fight of faith and know in your heart that we already have won; In Jesus' name.

After I got my driver's license back, I was so excited. I was giving God all the Glory and crying and praising God! Saying, God you are so awesome! I bought a car with the money I earned at my job. Wow! Look how God changed my life! What a turn around. God is so good.

After about 3 years went by, I took some Christian training classes. God was moving in my life and I was growing in the things of God. He was filling me up with the word of God. And watch this...after I did time in jail, God sent me right back to the same prison to glorify Him and to do prison ministry in the same place. I actually started doing bible study where I had been incarcerated. Wow, God is incredible. It was like a transformation; I was looking at the same cell I used to be locked up in. The guards were like, "what? How did you get back in here?" I told them, "God did it!" What's so funny about me being back inside was that you have to go through the system to get your fingerprints done. Only God could've done something like that. It was so powerful that people were yelling in the jail from the tiers saying, "Yo, what up J Bond?" I was like, "Jesus is Lord!" Then someone said, "but you were out there getting' paper and shooting dice!" I said, "I know, look how God changed my life." They said, "Wow, what a change!" It also gave them hope in jail, because they remembered how I used to be. It was very different even people of other faiths remembered how I used to be and they said it was good that Jesus changed my life around and they were very surprised too.

CHAPTER 7

Seeking and saving the lost

I was doing bible study in prison and people were receiving salvation. Salvation is the greatest miracle! That's the most powerful thing in the body of Christ is winning souls. The bible says we were saved by grace through faith not of ourselves; it's a gift from God. So we thank God for His grace and mercy. After leaving bible study at the prison, I went home to see my mom. She was proud of the fact that God had changed my life and what He has brought me from. She hugged me and told me she loved me and she said keep up the good work for God. I said, "Thanks, I will and I love you too."

Time had passed and the word was out on the streets that God had transformed J Bond's life. I wasn't the same person I was before. So people had to see me live it because it's more than just saying that you're a Christian; you have to walk the walk and talk the talk. The scripture says in I Corinthians 4:20, "The Kingdom of God is not in word, but in power." That means don't talk about it, be about it; be about God's business. DO things in power and demonstration and be led by the Holy Spirit and let your light show that God's power is really working in you.

I was going to church (two services), and I was becoming strong in ministry and the word of God was building me up. One day I was in church and God spoke to my heart and said go visit my younger brother out of town. So I left church and started driving and it was a beautiful day. The sun was beaming and it was about 70 degrees. Driving down the highway I was on my way to see my brother and I had a smile on my face, I was happy! When I got to my destination, I pulled into a corner store. I didn't know exactly where I was so I asked this guy, "Do you know Double D?" the guy said, "Yeah, he's right over there on Fourth Street in the projects." I said, "Ok." It's amazing how it made me think how you can get information from people and how I used to be out there living a destructive life. This made me think about how many people gave information about me. It made the work for the boys in blue pretty easy. Lol.

I continued my journey on Fourth Street and I went to see where my brother was located and when I got there, a crowd of guys were hanging outside. They were like, "Yo, what up baby? What's the deal? What's popping?" I had just come from church and I had on a suit and tie. I told them I came looking for my brother Double D. One guy said, "Double D, we know him, who are you?" I told him I was his brother. I wanted to check on my baby brother. They asked, "What's your name?" I said, "J Bond, but you can call me Brother Jerry." He called my brother on his cell phone and said to him, "There's this guy who says he's your brother, but he's got a suit and tie on and he looks like a cop." Now I'm here to tell you, that when God transforms your life, people can't even recognize you. It's so awesome how God transformed my life how I used to be out there in the streets wheeling and dealing. God rescued me from the power of darkness and brought me to the Kingdom of dear Son. He took me from one position to another. I went from Hood to Good!

So my brother said, "Yeah, that's my brother, tell him to come up." So I went up the staircase in the projects. I said "What's up man?" He said, "I can't call it." I said yeah man; I haven't seen you in a while." I said, "What are you doing?" He said, "You know me man, I'm going out with a bang." (You know how we talk in the streets; that cool stuff). I said to him, "I love you man, I don't want to see you get killed in the streets like our other brother did, Money making A.D." He said to me, "Man you know how it goes, hard to the head, no punking out!" I gave him a hug and while I was hugging him

I was praying over him at the same time. I walked off with a tear in my eye. I got back down the steps where the crowd of guys was hanging out and I got back in my car. I was praying and crying out to God asking Him to spare my brother's life and don't let him get killed like my other brother. God heard my prayer because six months later, my brother got locked up with a bunch of other guys. By God's grace, he's still alive!

As time passed, my brother went to court and my mother and I were there. My mom is a strong woman of God; she stuck by my brother's side. There's something about a mother; no matter what we go through, they will always love their children. People just don't know all that a mother goes through and it's also rough for a single mother to raise children while a lot of fathers are not there. A mother's job is never done! My brother ended up getting sentenced to three life sentences with a three million dollar bail!!! When that happened, it was a very trying time for our family, but God is on the throne even in the midst of that. I stayed in contact with my brother in the beginning and wrote him letters and prayed for him and God touched his heart and he received salvation and got saved. Hallelujah! God is so good! My brother also got baptized while he's in prison and has a mentor helping him and now God is using him to minister to other people and they see how Jesus changed his life. Now he's a light for Jesus Christ in darkness. For the scripture says, "Let your light so shine before men that they may see your good works and glorify your father which is in heaven." Matthew 5:14. The most powerful thing is to let your light glorify God by your actions, words and deeds. Wow! What a turnaround! My brother also received his high school diploma. I was so proud of him. There's simply nothing too hard for the Lord. All things are possible with God. My brother is also writing his book now, sharing his testimony how God turned his life around. God is so amazing! It's never too late; never give up on your dream in life. It's something valuable and unique vision placed inside every individual that God created. Whatever the gift that's inside you, is a beautiful treasure that God wants to use for His glory to touch other people's lives.

CHAPTER 8

The Shop

Now as I am living, I'm still working hard in the ministry. I also opened up my own business. It was called Niesha's Hair Braiding and Beauty Supply named after my oldest daughter Niesha. God blessed me with some finances and I started to buy a car then God spoke to me and said open a store. This older guy told me you can do it; all things are possible to him that believe, open your store. I went downtown to get my business license. I met the landlord of the building and gave him the money. He asked me what kind of business I would be opening. I told him I wanted to open a beauty supply and hair braiding store. What a combination! I gave him the money, he gave me the keys and the lease and I was in business. Then I asked the older man are you willing to help me? He said yes. So it was on! We got the truck and we went shopping to get shelves to put the beauty supplies on. I got a sofa, tv, mirrors, styling chairs, cash register, some pictures and a price gun. I went to NYC to the wholesale place to buy products; do-rags, hair brushes, relaxers, hair rollers, scarves, flat irons, wigs and hair bonnets. It was a blessing that my friend, old man John helped me put the shop together. It was very nicely done with the spirit of excellence. I had to believe God to send the right people to braid hair and God did it. He answered my prayer.

God sent three hair braiders; two from Africa and one from New Jersey; and they all were good hair braiders. One of them did micro-braids within five hours and the invisible braids within six hours. I had everything I needed and then I had a grand opening. My family showed up; my mom, daughters, brothers, and friends came to congratulate me. Niesha came to get her hair braided at the grand opening. We all took pictures and we had appetizers and punch. The grand opening was a huge success. Wow, God did it! How he saved me from going down the road to disaster and how I was created by Him to be a business man and I didn't even know it!

Shortly after the grand opening, I got the business phone turned on and people were calling to make appointments to get their hair braided and also to get hair supplies. I would answer the phone and say, "Niesha's Hair Braiding and Beauty Supply, how may I help you?" I listened to myself and I sounded very professional. It was the spirit of excellence and God gets all the glory! So people heard about the shop on the street by word of mouth and they were coming by to visit. Some were people from high school and some were from the streets. My family would come by to support me as well by purchasing hair products. I was doing well. I recall one time when my cousin called and asked if I had a certain type of weave with the color burgundy which is number 33. I told her no, but I would make sure that I'd get it within a couple of days. I had a good connection in NYC at the wholesale place. It reminded me of like being in the streets. God was using the same gift, but in a positive way. I was always being a go-getter. You have three types of people in the world; people that make things happen, people that watch things happen and people who wonder what happened. We have to be the ones to make things happen. So people continued to come to the shop. They would say congratulations, I'm proud of you. God has brought you a mighty long way. Now having a business, you have to be very diligent. For the bible says, the diligent shall rule. So you have to be a good steward over the things that God has given you. In business, you have to be persistent, determined and focused.

One day, while I was in the shop, God spoke to me and told me that the shop belonged to Him and that I was a vessel for Him. When people came to get their hair done, God told me to make sure that the atmosphere was right with praise and worship music. I did what God told me to do. When customers would come to get their hair done, they'd actually say that they could feel the presence of God with the anointing. There was a peace and calmness and also a lot of laughter and joy in the shop. When people got their hair finished and bought hair products, they came to the front to pay; they used to tell me that it was so peaceful in the shop. They also were impressed with how the ladies did their hair. Customers would say that they'd definitely be back. It reminds me when Jesus said if I be lifted up from the earth, I will draw all men unto me.

Some of my old home boys stopped by who remembered who I was before God changed my life. They said that the shop was put together nicely. It gave them hope; because now I was doing something positive with my life; instead of always doing negative things. There were things that was effecting me negatively like; shootings and muggings and out there in the streets going nowhere in life. The bible clearly states, "Where there is no vision, the people perish." Proverbs 29:18. So we have to have a vision in life, we have to have a goal and a dream. I heard someone say once, "The poorest person in life is a person without a dream." Your dream will make you rich and your gift will prosper you. I know a young man who came by the shop with my old home boys and he'd seen me open up my shop and how God had changed me. And about five years later, God gave him a vision and he opened his own store. Now that's a positive influence! The word influence means the capacity to have an effect on character, development or behavior of someone or something or the effect itself. So the presence of God that is on my life had a positive effect on someone else's life by changing him for the better.

CHAPTER 9

Changes and Challenges

*A*fter the shop experience, which was about five years, I moved to Virginia because of ministry to do God's will. We all know that His word is His will. I got a job as an officer writing parking tickets. I worked for about a year. To God be the glory my supervisor said that I was one of the best workers giving out tickets. I was always on time, had perfect attendance and was always willing to help others and I would stay over time even when it wasn't my shift. I would go above and beyond the call of duty. I went from getting tickets to giving out tickets. God is so awesome! He is so faithful and true to everything He does. After the year was up on that job, it was very interesting how I got my next job for my next assignment. We all know that the God we serve is the God of increase. Sometimes when we are working, we get frustrated with the work we're doing on our jobs, not knowing that it's a test that we have to go through to take us to the next level. The bible says, we go from faith to faith, to glory to glory. We go from one dimension to another.

I'll never forget as I was preparing to go to the next level, I met this lady and she was a driver at a well known community home. She was driving a big bus and I was writing tickets. God spoke to my heart and He told me to ask her if they were hiring. She looked at me and asked how I was. I told her I was doing well. I was looking for a new position and I wanted to work helping the handicapped. I asked her because she was driving that type of vehicle. She told me with a big smile, "By the way, we are hiring." I told her, "Ok, wow! That sounds good." I asked her what I needed to do to come get the job. I was walking in faith! She said, "You need to come by and fill out the application and take a drug test and bring your birth certificate and driver's license." She told me that they started at 12.50 per hour and that was more than what I was making at the time. God is so good and faithful to His word! The next day, I went to the place on my lunch break, filled out the application, went to take the drug test and waited. About a week later as I was praying every night and day, seeking the Lord, I received a call from the lady I met. She said, "I have good news; you have just been hired! We have orientation next week and we would love to have you. The pay starts at 12.50 per hour." I said, "Hallelujah, thank you Lord for the new job!" My steps are ordered by the Lord. God answered my prayers and I got my breakthrough.

I started my new job within two weeks, after I gave my old job two weeks' notice. It was very different from my former job with the parking tickets. I met a lot of new people and saw some new faces. I went to orientation and everything turned out well. I was still in ministry remaining faithful to God and my pastor. I encountered my first test on the job and it was with the women. I was challenged with strong seducing spirits. I was a new face in the place. I overheard the women saying, "Oh no, he's mine." Another one said, "We will see about that, its first come first served." They started chuckling and laughing. So as time went by, I learned my route and became very good at and I stayed focused. I met all the clients at the home they loved my spirit. I took them shopping, bowling, fishing, to the grocery store, to football games and to the park. I also took them to a popular amusement park. I met one of the clients who is also an author. God is good, there's nothing too hard for the Lord. If we believe, we shall receive the awesome things God has for our lives. That's why God says, "I know the plans I have for you, plans to prosper you, and not harm you, to give you hope and a future. Jeremiah 29:11.

As I continue on my job, the word is out that there's a new driver for the bus transportation department and he's a nice young man. I met different people, staff, maintenance department, etc. Those same women came back around again. One day I entered the lunch room and they crossed my path. I said, "Hi, how are you doing?" They said, "What's up?" I said, "I'm doing well, how about you?" They said, "We're fine." They started laughing again. I said to myself, "I wonder what the jokes about?" But in my mind I already knew. I continued to stay focused and I told myself I don't have time for distractions. I'm in ministry and God is preparing me as an evangelist preaching the gospel. So later that day after lunch, this guy comes up to me and said, "Yo, home boy, those women are really at you, I overheard them talking in the lunch room about you." I said, "About what?" He said, "They said that they are out to get you and you're fresh meat!" He said, "You know what I mean?" I told him politely and looked him square in the face between the eyes and said, "No I don't because I'm a man of God and I have to be faithful to God." He started cracking up and said, "Good luck," As he walked down the hallway." So as I continued to be persistent on my job helping the clients and also praying for them, you know, laying hands on the sick so that they could recover while I was working for the Lord Jesus.

A few months go by and things were going well at the home and my supervisor was very happy to have me on board. They said that my work ethic was great and God gets all the glory. So ministry is going well at this time and I went to church to let my pastor know what has been going on in my life with the women at my job. My pastor responded by telling me that he'd keep me in prayer. It's the testimony and the anointing is what they're after he told me. But, he told me to be steadfast and seek to honor God and that my reward comes from Him. I said, "Thanks, I needed to hear that." A few days later a young woman challenged me on the job. She asked me for my phone number and how she could get to know me better. I asked her, "First, what's your name?" She said, "Tracey, from Georgia and I have been here working for a couple of years and I have a son." I said, "Tell me a little more." She said, "I like to cook and go shopping." I asked her, "What church do you attend and are you saved?" Then she said, "Yes, I am saved and I grew up in church and I sing very well today." I said, "I'm in ministry being committed to God." Our conversation progressed and I asked her to visit my church. She said, "I will, what time does service start?" "Bible study is Thursday at 7:30pm and our Sunday service is at 11am. There is powerful praise and worship and the word of God is taught in power and demonstration," I told her. I Corinthians 4:20 says, "The Kingdom of God is not in word but in power." What that scripture is saying is, don't talk about it, be about it! She said, "Yes that's what I'm talking about." "Do you mind if I bring a girlfriend with me?" "I said, "Sure, bring her to enjoy the service."

So first they came on a Thursday night for bible study and she sit right next to me. Then she said, "I like the service a lot, and I will be back." So my pastor and first lady was like, "She's pretty and she is a nice young lady, we just have to see what the Lord says." I said, "Ok, I know but in my heart I knew that they would be praying that God's will be done, not mine. So the following Sunday, she came to church and she bought a couple of her friends too. We all were praising and worshipping God in the sanctuary, we were in God presence. The scripture says in Psalms 16:11 that God will show you the path of life and in His presence is fullness of joy, at His right hand are pleasures forevermore. After church, I went back to work that following Monday and boy she was telling everybody about the powerful service we had on Sunday. People also received salvation at the service. Her and her friends were talking about it too. The good news was spreading like a ripple effect and the seed was planted. God is good and His mercies endure forever. I was still staying focused, working hard and still conversing with Tracey taking it slow. I wasn't in a rush because the Holy Spirit doesn't rush. He guides and leads into all truth. I told her thanks for coming to service, she said, "No problem, it was my pleasure." I told her to come back again with no pressure and told me she would. A few weeks went by, she came out of nowhere and brought me some clothes and cooked me a plate of food. She said, "Do you like chicken, rice, corn and green peas?" I said, "Yes." She said, "Ok, I made some lunch for you, I hope you like it." I said, "That was nice of you, what a surprise, you are talented and gifted." She smiled. I received the gifts and the meal and I ate the lunch that she made for me. Of course I prayed first. I was surprised, the meal was good and I said, "Wow, she can cook." The weekend was coming up and I said, "Tracey, what are you doing this Saturday?' She said, "Not much, probably going out to the club for a little fun and some partying. You know what I mean, I got to get away sometimes, and you work with all that work drama." I said, "Ok, we all have a choice because there are consequences for what we do." I wasn't trying to condemn her or anything; I was just letting her know that I cared about her wellbeing. It's interesting how when you're getting to know someone how time reveals all deception. You also have to go through all the different seasons in life and get to know a person and their daily pattern, because your success is in your daily regimen. You have to find out whose voices do they have confidence in and whose voice do they honor. I would hope that it would be God and His word, because Jesus said, "My sheep know my voice and a stranger's voice they will not follow." Meaning they are following the word of God which is the truth. Its gets even deeper, some people marry for money and personality, you should marry for moral traits; because a person with morality can get money. The bible says that a good name is better than great riches and while you "dating," time and being patient will expose hidden motives. That's why patience is a secret weapon that forces deception to reveal itself. There are certain things that are hidden and you take your time to allow patience to have its perfect work. That is why you never know what you are dealing with because patience has to expose some things to you. Time will unveil and actually pull off the covers in a relationship; because the truth shall stand the test of time and a lie will be exposed. I have learned many lessons in relationships with women of the world and women of God and it's a big difference. You want a faith wife, not a fake one! He that finds a true wife finds a good thing and obtains favor of the Lord. Make sure you pray and seek God's face for the answer and make sure that your marriage is ordained by God. God knows everything; He's the Alpha and Omega, the beginning and the end. Before you were formed in your mother's belly, God already knew you and had a great plan for your life.

In the meantime, still working at the home, some curious thoughts came across my mind about Tracey. I was seeing her lifestyle and it was some worldly things going on in her life. I said to myself that I would have to keep her in prayer. Some strong, lustful spirits were trying to convince her to stay right where she was. In a low place! That's why living by faith is a lifestyle. We have to watch what we do for God because people are always watching us, to see if Christ is really living on the inside of us. The following week, I saw Tracey and asked her how her weekend was. She said, "Great, my girls and I had a ball!" I said, "Ok, that's cool." Then she pushed up on me and said, "What's up, let's go out and have a good time, maybe we could go to a little place to eat and relax and chill and get a room afterwards." I said to myself, I can't do that! I have to obey God. But, I have to be honest, my flesh was screaming saying, go ahead, it won't hurt anything, God loves you and all you have to do is repent! Huh! Wow! The enemy was trying to get me. He wanted me to fornicate seriously. I was even stressing a little bit, I have to keep it real. She was very attractive. You know how they say it in the 'hood, she was banging, a straight dime piece! I had one of my friends with me, a good brother in Christ at the time and I recall that when I showed him the picture of her, it caught him off guard. He laughed because he started lusting too! I said, "Ok brother, I see you're drifting away looking at her in the wrong light." He said, "Man, she's fly, a bag of chips with the dip." I said to him, "Man, you're getting in your flesh too aren't you?" I said, "Be honest, you would probably hit that and then ask

God for forgiveness and say Lord your mercies endure forever?" He just laughed. Then I said, "Don't you know there are consequences for the sins that we commit even though God have already forgiven us and that His grace is sufficient? We still don't want to do things on purpose because God knows us, we can't fool him, it's best to surrender all to Him and let God finish His good works in us; shaping and molding us into Godly men and virtuous women that we should be."

I responded to Tracey's request and simply told her that I could not do what she was asking of me. I have to live right and honor God in holiness. I believe she got offended and maybe even embarrassed. Because she said, "Oh, you must be funny or gay?" I was like. "What, now since I don't want to get involved with you, I must be gay, wow, that's crazy." The devil will try anything to get you! I said, "No I'm not gay, I'm a man of God who desires to obey God." I said to myself, the devil is a liar! So she walked away and says, "Whatever!" She was smiling while she walked away. After about a month goes by, my supervisor says that I'm doing an outstanding job with perfect attendance. God is good! So after I passed that challenge with Tracey, I never knew that God had a blessing for me right around the corner; because during my lunch one day, my director made an announcement in the middle of the hallway and called everyone to the center, employees and clients, and gave me the MVP of the month award and a big bonus check of five hundred dollars! Yeah, look at God! It's true; He rewards those who diligently seek Him. Hebrews 11:6. I'm telling you, when they called me for that award, I was startled and shocked! They took pictures of me and gave me a plaque. I was smiling from ear to ear and people were clapping and hugging me for my good deeds. Yes, God was watching and keeping track of everything as I was being tested. I spent three years in this position and within that time I had received raises and bonuses and my track record remained the same.

Chapter 10

The phone call

$\mathcal{A}$s things were going well on my job and in ministry, I get a phone call from my hometown in New Jersey and it's my brother saying that my mom wasn't doing well. She had to go to the hospital and have surgery. I said, "What happened?" He said, "I don't know, it just happened all of a sudden." I was shocked and confused, just in a daze while my brother was talking to me over the phone. He said, "Hey man, do you hear me?" I said, "I think I do." He said my name again, "Jerry!" I said, "Yes, I hear you, I'll be there, I'm coming, my mother needs me!" I said to myself, I can pray and stay here, but there's nothing like my presence being there with my mother. I got the bad report about my mother, but I was going to believe the report of the Lord! I believe that by Jesus' stripes she was already healed. For we just have to stand on the promises of God and put our confidence in God and believe that everything would work out fine.

So the first thing I did was let my Pastors and Elders know what was going on with my family situation concerning my mother and they would be praying because God is faithful and she will be fine. I told them, "Ok, but I'm going to see my mother and God put it on my heart to go back home and I also have to let my job know too; I know my supervisor is going to take it hard.

When I get to the job, I saw my supervisor and asked her could I speak to her in the office. She said, "Sure." I spoke to her in the office and I let her know that I had to go back home to New Jersey to see my mother and be with her for a while. She said, "Aww, I'm sorry to hear about your mother, we will definitely miss you here. You have made such a great impact with your work ethic, kindness and character, that it has left such a positive effect on this company. You are always welcome here." Her words had such sincerity that I started to cry in her office and she hugged me while I cried.

So I was on my way back to New Jersey, and I thought about how everyone I had met over the course of three years in Virginia had received the Christ in me by prayer, helping and encouraging and winning many souls for Jesus. Some of them hugged me and they even wanted to throw me a going away party, but I didn't have the time, I had to get home for my mother.

I got back to New Jersey within five hours. Some say it takes six hours; I had the pedal to the metal! I arrived at my mother's house; she was already at the ER. I went there and asked if they had her back, and they said yes, she was scheduled for surgery very soon. I said, "Ok, what room is she in?" They said, "she's in room 207 on the second floor on the left." I said, "Thanks a million!" I started rushing to the elevator and when I got the second floor, I went right to 207 and I saw my brothers, my aunt and my daughters and a few cousins. They said, "Hey brother Jerry, good to see you." I was like, "Good to see you too." I gave them a hug and asked them where my mother was. They said that she was sleeping right now because of the medication. So I walked in the room and smiled at her and the first thing I did was lay hands on her and prayed. I said, "Love you ma!" Even though she might have been resting, she still knew my voice. I had my bible in my hand and started speaking the Word over her body, declaring and decreeing God's promises and thanking Him for the victory in advance. Not long after I got in the room, the nurses came to take my mother to the operating room. When she left, I started making calls to my friends who are Pastors for much needed prayer. I was staying in faith no matter what it looked like in this situation.

After the prayers, I went downstairs for a cup of tea to calm me down a little. My mom was in surgery for about four hours or more. I had to admit I was a little nervous. Not scared, but nervous. So after the surgery, the doctor came and spoke to me and said that everything went well. She's a strong woman and she's going to be fine. I said thank you Jesus! Hallelujah, you're awesome God! So after she recovered, she spoke to me and said to me, "How did you get here?" I said, "Your sister told me that you were in the hospital, so I got here as soon as possible." My mother was trying to talk and move a little and I told her, "Stop moving so much and try to rest so God can continue His process of healing you. Just take your time, it will all come together, I love you mom." So a few days passed and the doctors said that she was doing better and that they would be releasing her in a couple of days. He said, "She will have to take some medication and follow a liquid diet, but otherwise she will be fine. We will just watch how everything unfolds." I told him, "Thanks doctor, God bless you, good job!" Believe it or not, we have doctors that are anointed by God too.

After about three weeks, my mother is now at home taking it easy and healing. People were calling to check on her saying to her that the doctor said that it was a miracle that she came through. Prayer is a powerful weapon; it changes things for the better! All during this time, I made an effort to spend time with my family; my mother, brothers and daughters and grandchildren as well. Yep, I am a grandfather, isn't that something! Now everything is coming together fine. I recall a time with my daughter Niesha and my mother's living room when I came into the house. She was sitting down watching t. v. sucking her thumb and playing with her belly button. I said, "Hey Niesha, how are you doing?" She said, "I'm doing fine." She was smiling as usual with her father's smile. I go to hug her and she says, "Get off of me, stop playing." We both started to laugh, joking around with each other. My grandchildren said, "Hi grandpa, take us for pizza and games." I said, "Ok, I will, when do you want to go?" They said, "Right now!" I responded by saying, "You have to ask your mother first." They asked her, "Mom, could we go, could we go, please?" Their mother Niesha said to me, "If you're going to take them, go ahead and do, don't tell them you are going to do something and you don't do it." And I said, "No, I'm going to take them." I believe she knew that God had changed my life, but she wanted to see me live it, not just talk it. She wanted to see my actions behind my talking. It reminds of me how Abraham had faith, but what made his faith complete was his actions. As a man of God, now I had to show her that Christ really changed my life and I was a new person, the old man was dead and gone. A couple of days later, I took my grandchildren out for pizza and games and boy did they have a good time. They played in the balls, in the tunnels and they played basketball and were eating pizza. All I kept hearing was, "Grandpa, I need more coins!" They were so happy that day and I just sat back and smiled watching them have so much fun.

So I came back from taking them for pizza and games and when I took them home to their mom, they were yelling her name, "Mom, we had a good time with grandpa, we had so much fun!" Niesha said to me, "You finally got what you wanted, they now call you grandpa." She smiled and said, "Thank you for taking them and by the way dad, let me get one of those t-shirts From Hood to Good, I'm feeling those, they're hot!" So I asked her what color she wanted so that I could bless her with one. She said, "Give me an orange one." It was a nice summer day and she put it on and started dancing in the mirror saying, "Ho, ho what's up, how you like me now?" I smiled and said to myself, that's Niesha for you.

CHAPTER 11

The Vacation

As I continue to have a very interesting time with my family, a few months later, I decided to take a vacation; a cruise in fact. Just to get away on some business and to focus on some visions and dreams that God had given to me. Everything was going well, the food was awesome! The water was so beautiful, it was turquoise in color. It seemed to be a great, relaxing vacation so far. I remember calling one of my good brothers on the phone letting him know I was on vacation. He said, "That's good man, we need to get away on vacation sometimes." I received a call in the middle of the night at about two-thirty in the morning from my mother's good friend's daughter. She said, "Your daughter has been in a car accident. She and the children were involved." I said, "What! What's going on?!" She repeats herself saying, "Your daughter has been in a car accident." I asked her which one and she said, "Niesha." I asked her how was she doing and she replied, "She's in the hospital having surgery and your grand baby has passed away already." Shocked, floored, stunned not a word I said; tears running down my cheeks; believing that this can't be really happening. I said, "This has to be a joke, please God help me, I cried! I recall at the time that I was trying my best to stay calm. I called a friend of mine who is a prophet and told him what happened; he started praying for God to supernaturally intervene. I let the people on the cruise boat know what happened concerning my daughter and they told me that I would be the first one that they let off of the ship when we got back to our destination.

The next day was approaching, and my daughter was still in surgery. Family members at the hospital said that there were over two hundred people there for Niesha and the family. People were praying and crying. My little grandson got banged up but survived, praise God for that! The next day comes and I call my mother and she told me to keep praying. A few hours go by and I called back and my mom tells me that my daughter Niesha just passed away and has gone to glory. I just dropped the phone and walked away in disbelief, holding my face in my hands with tears in my eyes looking at the water and the sun, waiting on a boat that I can't get off of. Right after that, pastors called me to pray for me to keep me in my right mind, because I didn't know whether I was coming or going. I said to myself, my faith as a man of God is shattered; I stood on the word of God, I believed it, I spoke it, what happened? At first I thought about Job and of King David and how their faith was tested and how Job lost his whole family and how God repaid him double for his trouble. So as I finally get off the boat and get into my car, I go straight to my mother's house and see so many people; uncles, aunts, cousins and friends. Everyone gave me a hug when I got inside saying how sorry they were for my loss. But in the midst of it all, I'm holding on strong, still giving God the glory because I know that I can rejoice because I know that my daughter and grand baby were saved and both are now in heaven. I even spoke to my daughter's pastor and he was telling me how faithful she was in church; I overheard that she never missed a tithe and she had a heart of compassion. She also took very good care of her children and loved them. So as I was speaking to her pastor, he asked, "If there is anything I can do just let me know." He also said that he would do the eulogy. I said, "God bless you and thank you so much." I also recall a time when a young man from the church came into my hair supply store called Niesha's, and he brought a few items which came to a total of about ten dollars. He gave me a fifty dollar bill and told me to keep the change. It's amazing that about five years later, Niesha went to their church and became a member. The scripture is so true, the bible says be not deceived, God is not mocked; whatsoever a man soweth, that shall he also reap. Galatians 6:7. Now that's a powerful testimony!

CHAPTER 12

The Celebration

*S*o after I had finished talking with the pastor, we all had to make preparations for the home going celebration. God always ends on a positive even when it looks like it's a negative, but I know God will get the glory! A few days passed and the day of the celebration came. So many people showed up that it had to be at least one thousand people there. Her pastor preached a powerful sermon and God used me to bring forth a word too. So many young teenagers came to the altar, gave their lives to Christ and got saved! Some of them were filled with the Spirit! God is awesome! Over one hundred people got saved that day. It was one of the most extraordinary moves of God amongst the younger generation that I've ever seen. Psalms 102:18 says.

"This shall be written for the generation to come; and the people which shall be created shall praise the Lord."

After the service, everyone gathered downstairs for the repast. I saw a lot of my good friends and some of my homeys from the streets. They showed me much love, telling me to be strong and that they were there for me. I said, "Thank you." I was rejoicing but my heart was still crying. I can no longer call my daughter or take my granddaughter out but I can rejoice at the fact that they are with Jesus in heaven. Absent from the body and present with the Lord.

Niesha attended several colleges for the Criminal Justice field and desired to be a corrections officer. She was also an excellent poetry writer and it showed in many of her writings. As a father, I desire to create a scholarship fund in my daughter and granddaughter's name in the near future; so God will get the glory!

So you probably are wondering what happens next right? Well, after some time passes, time doesn't wait for anyone. I eventually moved back to Virginia, married an anointed woman of God named Junita who is very dear to my heart; and that's where we're located in ministry evangelizing, spreading the gospel of the Kingdom of God. Helping the youth encouraging improvements in their lifestyles and letting them know that God has a plan for their lives and a purpose according to Jeremiah 29:11. Also, to let them know that they have big dreams in a big world to do big things.

Grace and Peace in Jesus' name!

If you are reading this and currently have not made Jesus Christ the Lord of your life, or perhaps you may have strayed away at some point in your life, you should consider rededicating you life to him today.

Although I am not personally in front of you as you are reading this, I want you to know that Jesus can come right into your heart where you are standing, sitting or laying right now. All you have to do is confess him and believe in your heart. Would you do that with me today?

If that is you, confess the Salvation prayer:

Heavenly Father, I come to you in the name of Jesus I pray and invite Jesus to come into my life. I renounce and repent of my sinful past. Jesus I believe that you died and rose again. So that I would be free to love, worship and serve only you because you have finally set me free! I can truly turn from my old ways and life for you. I am now born again.

I am saved according to your Word.

Thank you Jesus, for setting me free! It is in the mighty name of Jesus, Amen!

Personal Updates

I would like share with you some personal updates. In the scriptures, the bible says *therefore if any man be in Christ he is a new creature old things are passed away and behold all things become new*. I am a new person in the Lord today I have a new heart, a new mindset, now I go out and share the love of God from my life experiences.

If you are reading this and currently have not made Jesus Christ the Lord of your life, or perhaps you may have strayed away at some point in your life, you should consider rededicating your life to him today. Although I am not personally in front of you as you are reading this, I want you to know that Jesus can come right into your heart where you are standing, sitting, or laying right now. All you have to do is confess him and believe in your heart. Would you do that with me today?

If that is you, confess the Salvation prayer:

Heavenly father I come to you in the name of Jesus I pray and invite Jesus to come into my heart and be Lord and Savior of my life. I renounce and repent of my sinful past. Jesus I believe that you died and rose again. So that I would be free to love, worship, and serve only you because you have finally set me free! I can truly turn from my old ways and life for you. I am now born again.
I am saved accordingly to your word.
Thank you Jesus, for setting me free! It is in the mighty name of Jesus, Amen.
***

If you have received Jesus Christ today, I invite you email me at:
jjmiddle712@gmail.com

Final Thought:

Genesis 50:20 - *But as for you, you thought evil against me; but God meant it unto good, to bring to pass, as it is this day, to save much people alive.*

Your brother in Jesus Christ, *Gerald*

A Dedication and Prayer
to My Daughter

o Niesha and Aniyah,

I love you both dearly and I know that your life is now in heaven in the presence of God cheering me on to continue teaching the good fight of faith.

Who do I care what people think,

my thought is better than the rest.

Actually, God's though is better than the rest.

A book of words to adhere to,

something to trust when life gets you down.

Which one will you get –

sin, evil, drama, struggle, financial issues,

lies, pain, hurt?

When you miss it - it hurts you.

When you catch it you can change it.

Change is hard and gets the best of you sometimes.

Would you rather miss it,

or would you rather catch it?

by Niesha M. Middleton
1986-2011

To God be the Glory. Thanks be to God for his precious grace and <u>salvation</u>. "By grace are ye saved through faith; and not of yourselves; it is the <u>gift</u> of God" Eph. 2-8

In Jesus name, Amen